First Edition 2000

C000092358

This work may not be reproduced, copied or stored in any way
whatsoever without the permission of the publishers
except for brief extracts for purposes of review.

Published by Paul H. Crompton Ltd.
London & New York

ISBN: 1 874250 26 X

Printed and bound in England
by Caric Press Ltd.
Rickits Green,
Bearwood, Bournemouth,
Dorset BH1 9UB
(01202) 574577

Budo Masters

Paths to a Far Mountain

Michael Clarke

Paul H. Crompton Ltd.

Dedication
To the Memory of
Eiichi Miyazato sensei.
A rare and special man

Master Eiichi Miyazato, 10th dan
- late Headmaster of the Jundokan dojo.

Photograph - Stuart Fulton

Acknowledgments

It is with gratitude that I thank the masters found within these pages.

Their time, generosity and wisdom were given freely and patiently.

Without the spirit of giving from one person to another, the
essence of Budo could not survive,
and this book would not have been written.

I am indebted in no small way to the following people for their photographic skills and the use of their work in this book. I thank all those organisations and individuals for their permission to reproduce it here.

They are: Kevin Brennan of the Australasian Fighting Arts magazine, Sensei Sandy Starling, Sensei Jim Palmer, Sensei Robin O'Tani, Sensei Eiichi Miyazato, Sensei Jan De Jong, Paul Crompton, Norma Harvey, Fighting Arts International magazine, the S.W.K.U., my student Stuart Fulton, and last but certainly not least my wife, Kathy Clarke.

Opposite: Kanazawa Sensei demonstrates Kata.

Publisher's Note

Michael Clarke's first book, "Roaring Silence" was about his early experiences as a Karate student, and was especially interesting to readers who wanted to find out about those days when Karate was still relatively unknown compared with the situation today.

"Budo Masters" is about some of the teachers who fashioned not only the scenes of martial arts study which were being played out all over the world during the days of "Roaring Silence", and whose influence, now somewhat dimmed by the passage of time, still continues to play a part in the present martial arts world.

Every reader of this book will find much of interest and considerable inspiration within its pages. In particular the actual words of some of the masters about the meaning of 'style' and the ways of teaching a martial art should be very helpful, not only to more advanced students and teachers who will have thought about these subjects more than once, but also helpful to relative beginners who have observed things about their new art which at first may have seemed contradictory and hard to grasp.

Why does a style change? Should it change? Is it a 'bad' thing if it changes? Should we make efforts to ensure that it does not change?

These and similar questions are approached and answered by men who were in some cases present when the foundations of the art or style in question were being laid down.

Michael Clarke currently resides in Australia where he is still an active Karate-ka. He contributes to martial arts magazines and regularly-corresponds with martial arts students the world over.

CONTENTS

Preface

Within the following pages you will be introduced, maybe for the first time, to nine men who have spent the greater part of their lives walking the "Middle Path" of Budo; each in his own way. For more than two decades I have also struggled to make progress along a pathway that will I hope bring me closer to the place where they now stand.

In the East there is a saying, the exact rendering of which is difficult to translate, but it means that there are many different ways to the top of a mountain, but from the summit the view is the same for all. This is why those who have mastered a martial art, any martial art, are at peace with themselves; and not only with themselves, but with their fellow travellers.

When you have walked the Budo path for as long as the men who inhabit this book, the problems and difficulties which beset you as a younger person will seem insignificant. Nevertheless, they faced similar obstacles, and, as you will discover, nothing came easily to them. In reading how they dealt with these problems you will be able to take heart, as I have done, from their example.

There are several common threads running through the book. I advise you to take note of them, either through making notes or by physically copying them. The "Way" transcends all differences of gender, race or religion. So it is possible for anyone to embark upon a journey that may one day lead him or her to the top of that far off mountain that lies within each one of us; a mountain first glimpsed, perhaps, in our mind's eye when we first entered a dojo.

The order in which each Master appears in the book has no significance. The chapters are arranged simply to give the reader what I hope is an interesting, reflective and enjoyable walk through the world

of modern Budo. If we were to add up the experiences of training of all those whom you are about to meet, it would amount to more than four hundred and fifty years. Surely, we can all learn something from such an expanse, such a storehouse.

Remembering with the Body
Tatsuo Suzuki's Exploration of Pure Technique

Even today, with many people around the world calling themselves 'Master', there are still relatively few who can truly lay claim to such a title. One man who can is Tatsuo Suzuki sensei, 8th Dan of the Wado-ryu karate-do.

He was born in Yokohama, Japan, in 1928. He first became interested in the martial arts as a young boy, when the country was in the grip of military fervour. In 1942 he began his training in karate under the direction of a friend's brother. This was in a small back yard in the town of Hamamatsu where he was living at the time. The older boy was a university student in Tokyo, who returned each weekend. It was during these visits that the young Tatsuo and his friend were drilled in the fighting techniques of this 'strange' martial art.

Though he is not entirely sure today, Suzuki sensei believes that it was Wado-ryu that he was being taught, even then. He admits however that for the most part their instructor had them do little else but fight! His strongest memory of that training is just how rough the fighting was. Neither of the boys knew much about control or defence, and so each session ended with both of them covered in cuts and bruises.

I was intrigued that he had not started his karate training in a formal way, at a dojo, and asked him how and when he came to enter a dojo for the first time.

"I had been training with my friend in Hamamatsu for about two years and then I returned to Yokohama where I was born. Soon after that I began to look around for a karate dojo, and at the YMCA I saw a sign that said there were karate lessons taught there. That's when and

Tatsuo Suzuki sensei demonstrating Karate (1975)

where I started my formal training."

Suzuki sensei's earlier training paid off, because within the relatively short time of six years he reached sandan or third level black belt. As the Wado-ryu gave out dan grades at that time only as far as fifth dan, this was a very high grade for Suzuki sensei to have reached. I wanted to know what the early gradings or tests for dan levels were like, and how they compared with the gradings of modern day karate students. He said.

"I really can't remember much at all about my early gradings. Just like now, in those days I was not interested in grades or tests. All I wanted to do was train! Then one day I found myself at the dojo

wearing a black belt. After a while I was simply told that I was now a nidan (second level) and the same thing happened for sandan. The tests must have been concealed as it were in the usual training sessions because I don't remember as I said. I know that when I entered university I was already sandan. What I do recall well though is my test for godan (fifth level). In actual fact I thought that I was doing a test for yondan (fourth level) but it was for godan. In those days it was the protocol for your seniors to be graded up before you; otherwise you would be graded to the same level as those senior to you and in Japan at that time this was unacceptable. It seemed to me then that sandan was all right for me, that I was high enough, but some people from the university came to see me and asked me to please take the test so that they too could take the ones they were ready for. In Japan at that time if you knew that someone was better than you were, you would not grade higher than him. These people all knew that I was better than they were and so they could not move unless I did. Everybody was literally just waiting for me to take the test for Yondan. So I decided that I would do it, before I graduated from university."

"My test was under Ohtsuka sensei (the founder of Wado-ryu karate-do). When it was over he awarded me fifth dan. I was honestly very surprised and thought it must be some kind of mistake. If it were true, this meant that I had jumped yondan altogether. I went to Ohtsuka sensei and asked him if the award was correct. I said that I thought that it was too much and asked him to please give me yondan. He refused to do this and told me that the other seniors in the grading panel also thought that I should be godan. He said that I had to take it. This is why I can remember that test, because of this particular incident."

I knew from the research that I had done before meeting with Suzuki sensei that he held dan grades both in judo and bojutsu (staff fight-

Tatsuo Suzuki sensei demonstrating roundhouse kick (mawashigeri) on a speedball - (1975)

ing). I wondered how he had come to study these other arts. His introduction to bojutsu had come about because, "After the second world war we had to leave the police station building that housed our dojo. While I was training there Ohtsuka sensei was still young enough to do a lot of training with us. We spent many hours fighting as well as working on our kata and combination training."

"Ohtsuka sensei did all this with us at that time and the training was very hard. It was a good time to be at the hombu dojo because many old students were returning from the war. As well as these members we would always have visits from the senior students from some of the university dojos. They came to train with us quite often. But we

were told to leave the building and so we had to find a new place. Ohtsuka sensei came to us one day and told us he had found one."

"One of his friends, a Mr. Ueno, who was also a martial artist, had a dojo of his own. It was very small but as we could not find anywhere else we had little choice but to accept it gratefully. We trained there for about a year. Ueno sensei used to teach bojutsu as well as other martial arts. One day he asked me if I would teach karate there and in return he would teach me the art of bojutsu. In the end I studied other martial arts with him, even the shuriken (throwing knife or spike). He said that as I was doing karate, then the other arts such as bojutsu should not be so difficult for me since they all used plenty of hip action. So that's how other arts entered my life."

I knew that Suzuki sensei had made a study of Zen, and as this is a subject that had captured my own interest years ago, I asked him how this had come about and what instruction he had received. He told me that he had always been interested in the lives of the great martial artists from Japan's past. Even from his early days he had looked for books and read all he could about the way they lived their lives. He discovered that most of them had made a study of Zen, and so he decided that he would do the same. When he was at university, Suzuki sensei had been secretary of one of the Wado-ryu supporters' clubs. The patron of this club was a Mr. Tanaka, who was a very famous man in Japan at that time. He too was interested in Zen and had studied it under the guidance of Genpo Yamamoto, one of the better known priests of that era. Mr. Tanaka introduced the young Suzuki sensei to the priest, who in turn introduced him to his leading disciple, Soyen Nakagawa. Suzuki sensei takes up the story.

"Sometimes I would take a few of my karate students along to the temple, which was called Ryutaku-ji. Many years earlier, a very famous master of kendo (way of the sword) used to train in the temple grounds. I will tell you a story about him. One day a rival of his who was very strong and who had been beaten only once, came to the district. The master who trained at Ryutaku-ji temple wanted to challenge and defeat his rival, but knew that he could not defeat this man by technique alone; he needed more. Some kind of mental training was needed. At that time, Ryutaku-ji was also home to a famous monk and our hero decided he must go there and seek him out. He was living in Mushima, a small town some distance away. So every night he would ride his horse to the temple, study Zen, then ride back home. He did this for a long time, night after night, every night. The constant travelling was hard for him but he did it. Finally, one day, he achieved satori or enlightenment."

After that experience he lost all fear of his rival. He knew in his own mind that he could beat him. One day the two men met and our hero asked his rival for a duel. The challenged man took one look at his challenger and knew in his bones that he was already defeated. He acknowledged it. So this is Zen. This kind of thinking is very important in all martial arts and that is why I wanted to study it."

I enquired if Ohtsuka sensei had also approached Zen but according to Suzuki sensei he had not. Ohtsuka sensei had not been much touched by it at all. But in his later years Ohtsuka sensei would council his students to study Ochaku Zen.   This is a term used to describe simply lying down on one's back and closing one's eyes and then beginning to meditate. People call this the lazy man's Zen. When he thought about this advice of his sensei, Suzuki sensei wondered if the former knew more about Zen meditation than anyone believed. The more he thought about it, the more convinced he became that this was probably true. I asked him if he taught his own students any Zen meditation. He said that he did, occasionally. He explained.

Tatsuo Suzuki sensei at the Annual U.K.K.W. tournament (1980)
Photo - Norma Harvey.

"It's a little difficult to teach about Zen in just one or two lessons. If I am teaching on a gasshaku or training camp where everyone is together for a week or even longer, then I can do something. If it is only over a short time then I cannot get students to understand much. The thing about Zen is that you must do it yourself, by yourself, to find any kind of meaning from it."

I think that I understood what Suzuki sensei was saying. Perhaps this is why Zen and martial arts have always been lined together. Both disciplines have to be experienced to be appreciated.

"Zen", said Suzuki sensei, "is just like karate in the sense that they are both mental processes that should be done every day. And it is very important to continue once you have started."

Throughout our afternoon conversation the idea that karate like Zen is a mental training came up time after time. Suzuki sensei was full of little lessons that had the effect of making one think past the obvious. For example he told me how he had a training hall full of people and he sat them down and asked them who could walk across a plank of wood six feet long and one foot wide. Without hesitation everyone put their hands up. Okay, so how many could do it if the wood was two feet off the ground. Everyone could. Then he asked them if they could do it if the wood were one hundred feet off the ground. At that point, no one was willing to say that he could do it. He used this to show how the mind often sets limits on the body and the that the body could only surpass itself if the mind were stronger. After all, in the instance he quoted, the size of the plank had not changed; only the distance from the ground!

"To think of such things as this and to practise karate every day is very important. A famous ballerina once said that if she did not practise for one day, she could feel the difference in her body. If she did

not practise for two days, her partner could feel the difference. If she did not practise for three days, her audience could feel it. She said that this was why she had to practise every day, and I feel that way too."

In our days, Suzuki sensei feels that teaching is a much easier occupation than it once was. Over thirty years ago when he first left Japan to tour the West, he said he often felt that he had to 'show off' a little. When I asked why this was, he said that in those days when karate was still quite new in the West, people were looking for something which would impress them. For that reason, visiting teachers would give spectacular displays of fighting techniques against a knife or a chair attack. In a strange way this had meant that he himself had been obliged to train much harder, so as not to disappoint them.

Today, when people all over the world understand more about karate, he no longer feels the need to show off. Now he can help people to develop their character as well as their karate technique, and share with his students his own philosophy. But his drive for correct technique remains as high, and so his commitment to personal training remains high as well. I asked him, in view of his frequent travelling around the world, if he had found that karate was indeed developing character as well as technique, and if character development had become a more important factor. He said.

"You know, that all depends on who the instructor is. If the instructor has a good character then the students too will generally develop one, if they have not got one already. If they have not, then their character should change for the better as they progress with their karate. Unfortunately, in my experience, instructors with bad characters produce only bad students. This is because good people leave such instructors."

When not actually teaching or training, Suzuki sensei is never far from the subject which has dominated his life for over fifty-five years. For relaxation he can be found at his South London home reading up on any number of subjects; but perhaps it is no surprise to find he is most keen to read the words of his fellow countrymen from long ago. As he told me, "Most of these people have very good philosophies'. His other great source of relaxation is playing Japanese 'chess'. If doing neither of these things then it's a safe bet that he is watching a boxing video from his massive collection. He observed.

"I like boxing very much. I have most world champions on video and I like to watch them. You can see some really good moves from such people. You see boxing has developed very strong ways of delivering a punch, because they use only their hands. I think that in some instances the boxing punches are better than those of karate. A karate-ka might be able to defeat a boxer because he can kick as well, but if he could not use his kicks then the boxer would be much stronger. Boxing has a long history, so in our days it has a lot to draw upon."

This led our conversation on to the karate world's bid to gain entry into the Olympic games. I wondered if he had any views on this.

"I think is is about eighty per cent impossible. The reason is that taekwondo has already secured a place in the games. This was due in part to the chairman of World Taekwondo being a very clever politician. He is on the Olympic Committee and as you know he managed to have it included as an exhibition sport when the games were held in Seoul. They missed out in Atlanta but they are back again in Australia in the year 2000."

"To the public there is hardly any difference between taekwondo and W.U.K.O. style karate. So I think it will be impossible for karate to gain entry. If they did by some chance manage to do it I think the

publicity for karate would be a good thing; it would make things better than they are now. Also, countries would support their karate groups better than they do now, because they always look after sports that are in the Olympics better than the ones which are not. The other side of this situation is that if karate were accepted then more and more people would take up karate just for the sporting side of it. If this happened then I am sure that karate would lose its martial art content. This would be a bad thing."

As Suzuki sensei was speaking, I wondered how things would pan out in future. Would karate ever gain entry to the largest sporting spectacular the world has ever known, and if it did, would it, as he had predicted, lose its martial content in favour of the sporting ballet we see today. Whatever happens, I found myself hoping never to see the day when people put on a karate-gi (uniform) with the express desire only to win a gold medal. Returning to the question of personal training, I asked if hojo-undo (supplementary training) played any part in Suzuki sensei's own workouts. He said it did.

Wado-ryu Masters: Jiro Ohtsuka, Hironori Ohtsuka and Tatsuo Suzuki senseis - Photo Norma Harvey.

"Yes, I think this is essential. Wado-ryu movement appears to be very light movement with little or no power. But it looks this w a y because you have to stay relaxed when you are moving. When you hit your opponent though you have to have power, you have to be sharp. So hojo-undo training is important for developing this sharpness and power. But not too much weight training. The makiwara (striking post) is also very good for building your arms and wrists, as well as establishing good balance. It also helps you to develop a strong fist and achieve good focus."

In the closing months of 1991 when I conducted this interview, I knew that Suzuki sensei had formed his own world wide association quite recently. I was keen to know why he had taken this step, so late in life; why he had felt it necessary. I was not sure, for a moment, what his reaction to my question would be. I remember he reached out to the coffee table, picked up his cup and took a loud, slurping drink, in the way that Japanese people do to show that they are enjoying themselves. He sat back in his chair, and after a moment of careful consideration he began to tell me.

"As you know, after Ohtsuka sensei died, Wado-ryu in Japan split into two groups. I did not like this idea of two separate groups because I have always thought of Wado-ryu people as sisters and brothers. We are all, in the last analysis, Ohtsuka sensei's

Tatuso Suzuki sensei demonstrating elbow block and backfist counter (1968)

pupils. I have remained loyal to his Wado-ryu, and I am sure that he himself would not have liked to see two separate groups like this. I went back often to Japan to try to get the two groups to come together and make one association again, but this was in vain."

"I know the leading members of both groups very well. At one time I even thought that I had been successful in bringing them together, but I returned to England and shortly afterwards they had split up again. By this time I was really fed up with the situation. I really believed that if I had been living in Japan I could have done it. But the way things are I think there is no chance because they are always arguing with one another."

"As it is, I cannot ally myself with either group, as the senior instructors in the two groups are all junior to me. Only I have been training without a break since the days with Ohtsuka sensei. If the truth be told, most of them received their early training from me, so neither group has the experience which I have. I think this may be a reason why they keep changing the kata or the kihon-kumite (set exercises involving a variety of techniques). In this connection, I am a firm believer in what we call shu-ha-ri, which means to copy exactly, to extend and to make one's own, and thirdly to break away from. Shu means that everyone must do basic training, received from one's instructor, and do exactly as one is taught. So I am sure this implies that the basic kata and kumite of Wado-ryu should remain as Ohtsuka sensei taught them. But nowadays things are always being changed. Why? I consider that it is because the people who are making the changes did not train with Ohtsuka sensei for very long and so did not fully absorb the meanings. I was with him all the time that he was training at the peak of his abilities; that is, between 1950 until about 1965. During that period I was training with him almost every day. As he grew older he could not do certain techniques in the way he used to do them, but he did not change the techniques themselves."

"Today, most people cannot remember his true techniques and this is another reason why there are so many changes. People get together and discuss whether things were like this or like that. But shu is kihon, kata and kumite. You must keep pure Wado-ryu technique. I have a suspicion that I am the only one doing this now. When I made a series of videos a few years back, I invited the senior

Tatuso Suzuki sensei demonstrating a kneeling groin kick - Photo S. Starling.

Wado-ryu instructors in Japan to please come and watch them and give me their opinions. I asked them straight out, "What do you think?". They all said that this was pure Wado-ryu technique and Wado-ryu kata. These same people are unable to teach this way themselves because all of them stopped training sometime in the past and now they don't know which is the correct way. My own feeling is strong that I must teach Wado-ryu technique the way I learned it from my own sensei; in its pure form."

"During my time with Ohtsuka sensei I was training very hard as I said. I trained so hard that people used to call me crazy. Sometimes I would train for as much as ten hours in a day. As you see, I am not very tall or heavy and this influenced my thinking. It seemed to me that with my build, if I trained just like everyone else I would never be any good, never compensate. This was why I trained harder. It is through this hard, disciplined training that my body knows the right way to do pure Wado-ryu. It's not my mind, you see, that remembers, but my body; my whole body. Others are trying to remember with their minds and this is why they go wrong. But with me it's my body, because I have repeated the techniques over and over so many times."

"Now, if I belonged at the present time to one of the groups which was formed after the death of Ohtsuka sensei, and I said that the techniques should be done like this and like that, some of the seniors would be bound to disagree with me. The result would be that we would spend all our time arguing about the techniques instead of training ourselves. I can't waste time on arguing like that. But as I am independent I can teach my students pure Wado-ryu technique. So this is the long explanation of why I have formed my own group. I wish to stay loyal to my sensei and to the idea of shu."

"I held the opening ceremony in Japan for my new association. One

of the senior instructors from the Wado-kai (the larger of the two groups in Japan) came and gave a speech in which he said: 'I know that Mr. Suzuki is the only one who knows pure Wado-ryu tech-nique.' He also expressed the wish that even if the new associ-ation became very large that I would keep that purity. This echoed my own wishes and motives."

When Suzuki sensei came to live and teach in England, he used a number of locations in L o n d o n . Eventually he

Tatsuo Suzuki sensei demonstrating a backfist technique. Photo S. Starling

opened a full time dojo in Marvic House in Fulham. This was in April, 1979. Unfortunately by this time many of his students had moved on to do other things. Even so, the dojo was a great success. Quite often, visitors from Japan would come to the dojo and ask if they could train there and even teach. At that time, martial arts fever was rampant in the United Kingdom, indeed in the western world in general. More training sessions were needed and Suzuki sensei could not personally cope with all of them. So occasionally he would allow a visitor to teach some classes. Before this permission was granted, the person would be asked to fight with one of his English senior kyu grade students. These are students just below black belt level. Suzuki sensei remarked, "My students in England had a very high standard, and so yes, it was often sufficient to let one of these lower graded students fight the visitor. Remember that some of my students have gone on to become world champions."

I was interested to know who he considered to be his senior students now. He replied, "Well, there is Mr. Kobayashi. He was my assistant in England for about eight years. Since his return to Japan he has become karate instructor to Nihon University club. He also has other dojos. He is very loyal and I am proud of him. Both his technique and his character are good. This combination is something hard to find. Then there is Mr. Furakawa who acts as our general secretary, and Mr. Nagasawa also. They are both very good students. I also have some very good students in Australia and in America there is a group in Florida, and another in Venezuela. Some time ago the seniors from twelve countries came to Japan to tour and train together. They also made friends with one another!"

I knew from when I had lived in England myself that rumours about Suzuki sensei's departure to warmer climes had been circulating for years. Up until this writing he was, as far as I knew, still resident in London. I asked him about the rumours and what he felt about them.

He answered.

"Oh, yes, I would like to come and live here in Australia very much. The climate is so good, the people are nice too. But now my situation is this. If I came to Australia it would be difficult for me to travel, or for people to come and see me. I would be so far away from everyone else. I would have to send assistants to teach for me, but I want people to see pure Wado-ryu technique. This would mean spending more time with my best students, so once again this would mean a lot of travelling for either them or me."

Time was moving on and I had to bring the interview to a close. I wanted to know if there were any plans for a book. Suzuki sensei had written a number of technical books on his style. I was thinking more of a book about his philosophy. I pressed him on the idea of a biography.

He responded with, "Hm, that's a good idea. I haven't thought of that before. Yes, I would like to do it, if I could find a good writer to help... so if you come back to England I can tell you and you can do it." As I did not plan to return to England in the near future I thanked Suzuki sensei for the opportunity, then expressed my reservations at being ever able to take advantage of it. Still it was nice to be asked!

Suzuki sensei added, "But this is a good idea... maybe I should do it because I was always interested in the philosophy of the samurai of old, and the monks. You are right, I should do it. I will try one day."

My final question was more of a request. I was hoping that he would end the interview by imparting some advice to those of us who still have far to go. His answer was simple but profound. So often we students either forget or pay scant attention to the fundamentals of the martial art we practise. When we do this we are in danger of missing out on the storehouse of benefits our study can bring. But it starts at the beginning, on the very first day. Of all the things Suzuki

sensei could have spoken about, this is what he said.

"First, find a good instructor. If you do not do this first, then you will never learn good karate. Also, keep training once you have started. You cannot take time off from training. You must go all the time, and keep on going. Even people who are slow to learn will turn around and come to know karate, as long as they continue to train. So this is my advice to people."

With this our talk came to an end. I was sad that it was over. I could have spent all day listening to him. He is a charismatic figure and for a man his age, that is sixty-three at the time, the way he moved left me a little in awe of his abilities. Suzuki sensei is undeniably good at what he does and unquestionably knowledgeable about his Wado-ryu. As with every other master in this book, should you find yourself in a position to train under one of them then I humbly ask that you take my advice and do so.

Judo Saga
The Warrior Heritage of Robin O'Tani

There cannot be many westerners involved in the martial arts today who can trace their ancestry directly as far back as Robin O'Tani sensei. His lineage flows to the samurai of old Japan. He is a 5th Dan in judo and president of the British Judo Council. Born Jonathan Robin Masutaro Mortimer O'Tani, now known simply as Robin, he entered the world on January 3rd 1944 in Acton, West London. His mother Phillipa came from Streatham in South London, and his father Masutaro, as the name suggests, came from much further afield. In fact, his father was none other than the famous judo sensei Masutaro O'Tani, 8th Dan, a man whose name would have to be included in any history of judo in the West.

When Robin and I first met, I had intended to talk with him about his own involvement in judo, and that alone. But as the conversation developed, I knew that I would also have to include information about his father. Furthermore, the name Kenshiro Abbe, 8th Dan, cannot be left out either, as he was the teacher of Robin's father. To give our story a proper beginning however, we must go to the city of Nagasaki on the southern tip of Japan...

The Meiji Restoration in the latter part of the 19th century may have been seen by some as the emergence of Japan into the modern age, but for all that, many Japanese families found that the new era brought nothing but uncertainty and upheaval. Things did not all change overnight, and in addition to the major events such as the Satsuma rebellion, many single families had their own internal struggles and divisions. One such was the clan led by Robin's grandfather.

On a fateful evening when the rain fell softly on the sloping thatched

Robin O'Tani sensei, 5th dan
Photo - Michael Clarke

roof of the O'Tani family home, the clan 'elders' gathered together to finally settle the direction which they would collectively take. Elders they were in terms of seniority, but in years, some of them were little more than children. It was a samurai family, and it was vital that they understood and agreed about their position in the new order of things. Some were in favour of shaking off the past and moving quickly and boldly forward, just as their ancestors had done on the field of battle. Others were totally opposed to any further changes. They felt that the samurai as a whole had already conceded enough, including the loss of the 'top knot' of hair and the ban on the carrying of the famous samurai sword. Thus, lines were clearly drawn between the family members. They were split down the middle.

Robin's grandfather, eldest son of the deceased clan chief, had the duty to decide and make the final choice of direction. All the men of the clan sat in a large circle and took it in turn to air their views on the matter. Long into the night the arguments continued, from both sides, with neither giving ground in any way. As time passed, the atmos-

phere became more and more heated, and in the early morning hours tempers frayed. The long hours had charged the room with emotion from the powerful characters putting forward their views. During a particularly hot exchange, one of the men hurled an insult at Robin's grandfather, and his father, only fourteen years of age at the time, could take no more. He leaped to his feet, rushed to a small alcove at the end of the room, and snatched up one of the family swords from its stand. It had been his uncle who had pronounced the insult, and the youngster raised the weapon above his head and lunged at him. The cutting edge missed its target by the smallest of margins, whereupon Masutaro turned and made a second attempt to strike his uncle.

By this time everyone was on their feet, and pandemonium broke out. Masutaro's father yelled at his son to put the sword down but his son was heedless of the command. He was blind with rage, swinging the blade at everyone who approached him. Gradually he drove everyone from the room, and only then did he begin to calm down. All the family members, including his father, left him alone until the following day. It was then, in the cold light of day, that Masutaro realised what he had done, and faced his parents with that knowledge, as indeed he faced himself.

He had placed his own father in a very bad position. The son's actions had caused the father to "lose face" in the eyes of the other clan members. Some of them argued that if Robin's grandfather could not control his offspring then he could hardly be responsible for the control of the clan, and the destiny of the families who made up that clan. Within a year, Masutaro left school and ran away from home. He went to sea, working as a 'grease monkey' on several old, rusted up trading ships. The work was very hard, and often dangerous. His job was to keep the engines in working order, apply grease and oil to the moving parts and stay clear of the spinning drive shafts and other pieces of equipment. There was an element of danger in this part of his work and a false move could have resulted in very bad injury or death. Though the vessels he worked on travelled to different parts of the world, he saw little of the sights as he was mainly below decks.

One port of call was Ceylon or Sri Lanka as it is now called. Once in 1917, when he was able to go ashore on that island, his judo career began. For it was here that he met a fellow Japanese by the name of Seizo Usui. It is not clear whether Usui was teaching judo full time or if he made his living in some other way. Nevertheless he took Masutaro under his wing and started him off on a path he was to walk for the rest of his life. Whenever the youngster was in port, student and teacher would meet and train as much and as long as possible. As Masutaro's appetite for judo grew he spent less and less time at sea.

For some reason, Robin's father decided that he wanted to visit England. He never explained why but it was a dream or wish that he was about to fulfil. For two years prior to his visit he studied English language from a local village elder. Unfortunately for Masutaro the English he was

Kenshiro Abbe Sensei 8th dan judo - Martial Arts Supremo! - Fighting Arts International magazine.

O'Tani sensei demonstrates shoulder lock on a pupil.

O'Tani sensei showing hip throw. - Ogoshi

learning was not the language he would find on his arrival, but a 'pidgin' English which was spoken locally. It was a sort of 'slang' and so far removed from its mother tongue as to be described as a different language altogether.

The contact with judo which he made in Ceylon was not his first. Like many Japanese of his age, Masutaro had been introduced to judo and kendo (swordplay) at school. It is known that he first started to train in kendo, but gave it up soon afterwards because of undue bullying by the older boys. At this time he did not take judo at all seriously. But the seed of the art had been planted, so that when he resumed his study it grew large enough to consume not only himself, but future members of his family.

O'Tani sensei completing spring hip throw - Hanegoshi

In the summer of 1919, and now in his early twenties, Masutaro landed in Liverpool on the west coast of England. As soon as he landed he felt in his heart that he would stay in this new country, and indeed he never went back to sea again. Once he had found his landlegs he moved from Liverpool to London. Here, in the capital, his judo training continued in earnest. He began training under Hikoichi Aida Sensei and it was through him that he met perhaps the most famous of all the Japanese martial artists of the time, Yukio Tani Sensei. Although Tani Sensei is remembered in our days more for his act on the stage of Edwardian theatres, he was at the same time a gifted and well trained jujutsu-judo man. It is noteworthy that at this time, during the 1920's, that the distinction between judo and jujutsu was not so clearly drawn as it is today. In books of the period the words judo and jujutsu are used to refer to the same thing.

His meeting with Tani confirmed for Masutaro that he had found the sensei he wanted to follow. For the next five years he did just that. In 1926 he was appointed assistant instructor under Tani Sensei at the judo club which was to become perhaps the most famous in Europe, the Budokwai in London. It is usually regarded as the home of English judo, and was founded in 1918 by the famous judo-ka, Gunji Koizumi.

During those early years, Masutaro O'Tani became resident instructor for judo to both Oxford and Cambridge universities. All this took place under the banner of the Budokwai club in London, which was a main centre for judo outside Japan. Although the dates of O'Tani sensei's gradings are now lost, it is known that he received his shodan, nidan and yondan grades (first, second and fourth black belt awards) from his teacher, Yukio Tani Sensei. His sandan (third black belt rank) was awarded by Master Suichi Nagaoka. In his book 'The Art of Ju-Jitsu - The Practice of Judo', the well known writer and early British Budo-ka, E. J. Harrison, describes Nagaoka thus: "One of the greatest exponents of the art." The fact that Nagaoka Sensei was one of the few people ever to receive judan (tenth degree of black belt) would seem, to put it mildly, to confirm this statement.

In 1932 O'Tani sensei began to instruct at the Anglo-Japanese club in London. This remained his main outlet as a teacher until the building was destroyed in the German blitz of World War 2. During the same war he taught the Home Guard and the Metropolitan Police his judo and self defence skills. Throughout this long period of teaching in England he was very much the amateur as far as money was concerned. All he asked for were his expenses. He felt very strongly that he wanted to show the British people that there was something 'good' about Japanese culture.
In the daytime he earned a living as a fitter, having served a full engineering apprenticeship following his arrival in London. In 1938 he married a local girl and together they set up home in the Ladbroke Grove area, a district now famous not only as a centre of the antique trade but also for the internationally known Notting Hill Gate Festival. Within the year their first child was born. They named him Tomio.

The war years were not a happy time for anyone, and living in a country which was at war with his homeland did not help Masutaro at all. Matters came to a head one day when he was looking for a change

of jobs. Like everyone else during the war he had to work long hours, he also had a family to support, and was constantly on the lookout for more cash. He had heard about a factory somewhere else in London which was paying more. He managed to get time off work to go and look for the place. As he did not speak English very well, to find the location of the other factory proved quite a problem. As he was a foreigner, people did not feel inclined to help him, and finally he got completely lost. Someone became suspicious of him - Watch Out There Are Spies About was a typical wartime slogan - and reported him to the police.

O'Tani sensei was arrested that afternoon on the grounds of suspected espionage and within days found himself interned on the Isle of Man. The island had been transformed from a holiday destination to a prison for selected foreign nationals. After a few more days the charge of espionage was dropped, but the authorities persisted in detaining him, saying that he was an 'undesirable alien'. The detention lasted three months, then he was released. He said later that it was an experience he would never forget and numbered it among the darkest days of his life. It had been largely due to the efforts of his wife Phillipa that he had been granted freedom; without her he would probably have spent the entire war behind barbed wire. She had contacted the different groups of judo students whom her husband had taught during the two previous decades in England. Good references and messages of support came pouring in from all over the country from bodies such as the Police and Home Guard, professors from Oxford and Cambridge universities, and many individuals whom O'Tani sensei had instructed at the Budokwai and elsewhere. This culminated in a petition for his release being drawn up and presented to the Home Office. Then he was free. Though several weeks elapsed before a decision was made. So three months after he had set out on the fateful day merely to find a new job he was returning home. He was considerably relieved as one might expect.

The end of the war in Europe and the Far East brought changes for many, and O'Tani sensei was one of them. He opened a small dojo that was to become one of Britain's best known. It was called the Jubilee judo Club. He trained hard and taught hard, often being obliged to wring the sweat out of his judo-gi at the end of the evening. Not long after the war, in 1949, the British judo Association was formed. Most if not all judo clubs joined the BJA and O'Tani sensei was asked to become one of the new Association's senior instructors. It was a position he was happy to fill. In the period following this appointment he met many world famous masters of judo; men such as Kabumoto, Ishiguro and Kotani Sensei. These judo-ka came from Japan, and Master Ichiro Hatta of the Kodokan, Tokyo, awarded 5th Dan grade to O'Tani Sensei whilst he was teaching for the BJA.

By the late 1940's things were not looking good for O'Tani sensei. The British judo Association was doing well but O'Tani sensei's long time friend and teacher Yukio Tani Sensei had suffered a stroke and was no longer able to take care of himself. He died in 1950 and O'Tani Sensei became more and more frustrated with some of his students who, it seemed to him, were doing their best to Anglicize judo. He also felt that they had failed to support his sensei during his illness and by their actions had displayed a failure to understand the ways of Budo. Things came to a head in 1954, and in an effort to keep judo running along the lines he thought were right O'Tani Sensei left the British judo Association and formed his own group, the Masutaro O'Tani Society of judo.

The following year, the London judo Society brought to England a Japanese instructor who was to have a profound effect on O'Tani Sensei. He was Master Kenshiro Abbe, 8th Dan. Although the London judo Society was a club which belonged to the BJA and O'Tani Sensei was no longer with them, he made contact with Master Abbe, and felt at once that here was a man who he could respect and learn from. Master Abbe was however under contract with the London judo Society, and because feelings between them and O'Tani Sensei were not the best, the contact between the two Japanese men was slight for the first year or so. Then something happened between Master Abbe and the London judo Society which caused the Japanese to leave the club and form his own group, which he named the British judo Council.

Soon after, Master Abbe contacted O'Tani Sensei and the latter responded, taking every opportunity to train under him as often as he could. The two men found that they worked very well together. O'Tani felt that he belonged under Master Abbe's direction in quite a natural and simple way. As this was the way things were tradition-ally done in Japan, both men felt at ease in their respective posi-tions, even though life styles were different in England. In their eyes, this was how things had always been done and always should be done. By 1958, O'Tani Sensei had become national coach to the British judo Council and found himself wandering from place to place in Britain, teaching judo, much as he had done before.

In 1963 Abbe Sensei and his British judo Council were responsible for the largest display of Japanese martial arts ever seen in England up to that date. On Saturday, 23rd November in that year, in the Royal Albert Hall, London, demonstrations of judo, kendo, Aikido and Karate-do were staged by some of the highest ranking martial artists in Europe. As well as displays by Abbe and O'Tani Sensei of judo, the was Naessens and Stas Sensei from kendo, Nakazono and Noro Sensei from Aikido and Michigami and Harada Sensei from Karate-do.

The BJC grew from strength to strength and in 1964 O'Tani Sensei became vice-president. Five years later when Master Abbe stood down from the post of president, O'Tani Sensei was elected to take

his place. The following year, he amalgamated his own judo Society with the British judo Council. He had come a long way from being a ship's grease monkey.

Masutaro O'Tani Sensei was a man with very traditional views as far as the martial arts were concerned. He saw the study of judo as very much a way of life; something he had in common with the founder of the Budokwai judo Club, Gunji Koizumi. He did not believe for example in strict grading syllabuses. He considered that a new grade should be awarded not only for technical excellence and fighting ability on the mat, but should also include assessment of a student's behaviour and manner.

Of his own judo it is said that he was remarkable, both in standing techniques and groundwork. He believed strictly that a student should follow his sensei. This is what he had done, and he expected the same from his students. He died in January 1977 whilst on a weekend training course in Nottingham, England. He was teaching judo at the time...

When Robin began to tell me about his early days of training in judo I expected he would have much to say about his father. Time after time however he spoke of a man of whom I had heard very little about. Every time he mentioned the man's name a gleam would steal into his eyes and it became clear to me that I too would have to find out more about this man. His name was Kenshiro Abbe, the teacher who had impressed Robin's father so much.

Today, Abbe Sensei is remembered with great affection throughout the British judo world. He arrived in 1955 to take up his position as chief instructor at the London judo Society. He was then in his early forties and held a 7th Dan in judo. He was known for his textbook application of techniques, even during randori (free fighting). His training had begun at the Butokukwai in Kyoto, Japan. This organisation was founded in 1895 as a place to study all the Japanese martial arts. As new martial arts appeared and proved themselves, they too were taught at the Butokukwai. As well as the older arts such as kyudo (archery), judo and aikido and karate-do were part of the curriculum. Even arts such as swimming, climbing and flower arrangement could be learned there.

Abbe Sensei started his training as a young boy and by the age of fifteen he had already gained his Shodan (1st Dan). He went on to become the youngest ever 5th Dan in judo, reaching that level in his early twenties. Such was his martial arts prowess in general, that when he was studying kendo he was awarded Sandan (3rd Dan) at his very first grading or exam. Later on he took up Aikido under the Founder, Morihei Uyeshiba, and achieved Rokudan (6th Dan) level. It is also on record that he studied kyudo, karate-do and ju-Kenjutsu or bayonet fighting. In every art he undertook he gained high grades.

Within days of his arrival in England, the British judo scene was buzzing with stories of this Japanese master who he come among them. Abbe Sensei was a real champion on the mat, and had won almost every judo tournament held in Japan. At five feet eight inches in height, and weighing around 154 pounds he was every inch a judo man.

His abilities did not seem to diminish with age, and Robin told me that he would often finish a class by taking on a line-up of students. This is a common judo term for fighting the whole class, one at a time! According to Robin, Abbe Sensei could handle his students as though they were babies, even though in reality most of them were

much bigger in build and weighed considerably more than he did. When engaged in groundwork, opponents fared little better against him than they did standing up. It was said that he could use his feet like an extra pair of hands.

Though many believed him to be a 'natural' martial artist, and a natural judo-ka in particular, Abbe Sensei himself firmly maintained that he was not. He told Robin many times that his skill had cost him much in both pain and exhaustion over the years. He knew that his training was hard, but considered it necessary, for it was only by training hard that his efforts could help him live his life. Given this deep feeling for the martial arts, it is not surprising to find that he developed his own personal philosophy which he termed 'Kyushindo'.

The philosophical side of his teaching was seen by him as vital to the realisation of good technique. Only by understanding the philosophy and then applying its principles to judo and to life could one really benefit from one's training. An explanation of the term Kyushindo helps to show more clearly Abbe sensei's feelings towards his training and the role it played in his life. 'Kyu' means to investigate or to study. 'Shin' means the truth, the mind that comes from within, from real understanding, without ego. 'Do' means the way, as in way of life. So Kyushindo's message was to search for the truth within yourself, as a way to live your life. To some this may seem a very lofty ideology, lending itself more to the esoteric world than to the problems of modern day life. But Abbe Sensei believed that it was exactly this kind of thinking and the feelings that stem from it that would help a person to live and survive in the society which we have today. On a practical level, the principles of this philosophy ensure that should a person be able to apply them, he or she will have techniques of their chosen martial art which will work every time. The three main precepts are:

All things in nature are in a constant state of
motion. This is known as 'Banbutsu Buten'.

The motion is rhythmic and flowing.
This is known as 'Ritsu Do'.

All things work and flow in perfect harmony and
accord. This is known as 'Chowa'.

To go any further into the philosophy of Abbe Sensei would require several chapters, but the above synopsis may help readers to perceive what calibre of man we are speaking about. His influence on many martial artists in the western world was profound, particularly upon judo-ka.

It is not hard to see the origins of Robin's gentle manner and deadly skills, given the influence these two men had on him. I say deadly because I have felt first hand the pressure of his grip around my throat, and was left in doubt about the outcome of that encounter had I not tapped my leg as a sign of surrender!

Robin's training in judo began at the age of six, and as one might expect he trained first under the guidance of his father. This was at the Jubilee judo Club.   He readily admits that at this stage he was not very serious about training and saw judo more as a chance to play rough-and-tumble than learning a martial art. By 1957 however, as a boy of thirteen, he began to take things a bit more seriously and it was at this time that he made up his mind to make judo his life long study. As a member of his father's association he began to compete against older boys and on occasion with adults. Two years later and with the backing of his father, Robin joined Abbe sensei's British judo Council. Although his father's group and the BJC were working

closely together it would be a little while yet before they joined forces.

By the time he left school in July 1960, he was graded to 1st Kyu (the rank just below black belt). In August of that same year he passed his examination for Shodan and was presented with a black belt. It was during that same summer Gasshaku (training camp), a few days after his judo Dan grading success that he gained 1st Kyu rank in kendo. This was a great start to his martial arts career and in September, just one month later, he began employment as full time secretary for the BJC, and at the same time became personal assistant and personal student to Abbe Sensei. Robin admits that this was a great time in his life; fresh out of school, with all the time in the world to train with his Sensei, and at the weekends to travel around England acting as Abbe sensei's assistant. Everything went well until the day his Sensei was invited to do a teaching tour of France.

As the date for departure to France drew nearer, Robin became more and more excited at the prospect of his first overseas adventure. Shortly before the trip began, he was called into Abbe sensei's office and informed by his teacher that he would not be going. He was then asked to make the travel arrangements for Abbe sensei's new assistant. As he left the office, Robin was close to tears. Why had his Sensei done this to him? He had worked hard, trained hard, and up until now there had been no suggestion that anyone other than he would be making the trip. His upset turned to anger, and although he now looks back on the event with different feelings, at the time he remembers how hurt he felt. Abbe Sensei had explained things by saying that he needed to leave behind him in England someone he could trust to take care of things. But once left behind alone Robin began to brood over what he perceived as an injustice. When Abbe Sensei returned, Robin resigned from his position as secretary and dropped out of judo training altogether.

Soon after he began a five year apprenticeship as a tool maker. As a form of diversion he even joined a pop group. But nothing captured his enthusiasm and imagination as much as had judo; within a year he was back on the mat, training hard. He returned with a burning desire to prove himself, and to this end he would be found training six or seven evenings a week.

In 1962 he entered the first, and last, British Open Olympic Trials at Crystal Palace Sports Centre, London. Today, only members of one particular group can try out for the team, but in those days judo was new to the Olympics, and so judo-ka from the three main groups in Britain were allowed to send three people for each of the weight categories. Robin was one of the representatives sent by the BJC, hoping to enter the team. Unfortunately he did not make it into the National squad. The trials were fairly conducted, but no one from any group other than the British judo Association were successful. No one could match the fighters from this association. Afterwards, Robin recalled that he had been totally overawed by the occasion, and impressed deeply by the judo-ka from the BJA. Soon after the event he began to train at the Budokwai, very much against the wishes of his father. Over the ensuing months the situation strained their relationship considerably. Robin had no wish to hurt this father's feelings - he had nothing but respect for him - but the difference in training was a powerful draw on the young man.

At the Budokwai he could train with judo-ka such as Brian Jacks and Angelo Parisi; men whose future exploits would later make them household judo names. He felt that his exposure to such skill as such men possessed was beginning to pay dividends. Fatefully, it was just at this time that he was stricken with the bane of all who practice judo: cartilage problems.
As is so often the case, the remedy was to remove some cartilage from his knee. The consequent break in training brought him back

from the brink of confrontation with his father. So it is an ill wind... By the time that Robin had returned to normal training, his ideas and dreams of Olympic glory had been relegated to the back of his mind.

The year was 1965, and as a means of strengthening the spiritual side of his interest in martial arts, he joined the Aikikai of Great Britain (one of the chief Aikido groups). His judo grade at this time was Nidan (2nd Dan). His instructor in Aikido was Kazua Chiba sensei. But due to his other commitments this training lasted less than a year. In 1966 his hard work and dedicated efforts in judo paid fair dividends and he was grade to Sandan (3rd Dan) in the summer of that year by Abbe sensei. Not long after this happy event, another happy event arrived; he met his future wife, and within three years they were married.

Although his is now the president of the BJC, he had never seen himself in this role. Indeed, when it was put to him following the death of his father, he accepted the position reluctantly, and then only at the insistence of the senior members of the Council. Robin had always thought that his elder brother would become president, because he was after all, to quote Robin's own words, "A much stronger and more knowledgeable judo-ka than I". Tragically his brother died in a traffic accident. Had he lived he would undoubtedly have become the president of the BJC.

Shortly after his father died, Robin and his now growing family moved to Devon, in southwest England. Since that time he has tried to keep alive, with the help of other members, the principles and philosophy of Abbe sensei and of his father. He believes that these two strands should be the driving force behind judo practice. This has meant that a veritable educational system is in place; one that is both physical and spiritual; that ensures the growth of all those who follow its path.

Robin is a big man. His size could have persuaded him to rely on brute strength, but such is his appreciation of the teachings he has received that his actions remain smooth, flowing and gentle.

"The study of judo should be the study of life," he said to me when I met him. For Robin I believe it is. Could it be anything less, coming from such a rich judo background?

Masutaro O-Tani,
8th Dan Judo -
Photo Robin O'Tani

One Hit, One Kill
The Power and Grace of Shigeru Kimura's Karate

Kimura sensei in characteristic
Shukokai posture - S.W.K.U.

The first time I saw Shigeru Kimura sensei I was a fresh faced young man of 3rd Kyu (lowest level of brown belt). I had no more than a couple of years of karate training behind me. I had heard so much about him, but so far I had managed to see only one Japanese actually doing karate, and as yet had never managed to train with a sensei from the east. Like many other people training that time I ingenuously thought that all Japanese were small. I thought that all Japanese people did karate, and I further thought that all Japanese people were, or at least had been at some time in their lives, Zen monks! Such are the illusions of youth and ignorance...

On the evening I first saw Kimura sensei, all my dreams were shattered. He was six feet tall, for starters. He was a traditional Japanese sensei, but, he was equally likely to be thinking about karate in scientific terms.

On that summer's evening, when I was standing in the third row from the front, heart pounding and palms sweating, I knew I was in for an experience of a lifetime; something I had never experienced before. I was right. His warm up drills were unlike anything I had done before. Similarly, the way we did kihon waza was different also. Shoulders were to be relaxed, arms relaxed, hips relaxed. The fist went out in the manner of a fly fisherman casting his line. All the while he spoke of introducing shock power into the body of an imaginary attacker. Later, when the lesson moved on to working with a partner, I was asked to hold on to a thick foam striking pad while Kimura sensei demonstrated how to bring out the shock power he had been talking about all night. With both punches and with kicks his demonstrations illustrated clearly his ideas. As the recipient of his techniques, all be it through the medium of a protective pad, I was left in no doubt about their effectiveness, or his ability to deliver a shock. I was happy to experience that he produced just enough shock to prove his point. In the years which followed I have come across other teachers who were less willing to leave it at that. Kimura sensei was nothing if not confident about his ability. This confidence allowed him to be humble, and it was this humility which was, I think, his ultimate strength.

He had many students in countries all around the world. Indeed my next meeting with him was to be more than fifteen years later in Melbourne, Australia. This was half a world away from the small dojo in the northwest of England where I had worked so hard as a 3rd Kyu to keep up with my seniors and worked even harder to absorb Kimura sensei's technique.

Late in November 1991 I was on board a jet bound for Melbourne from Perth, wondering what the next four days would bring. I was on my way to meet Kimura Shigeru sensei, 8th Dan. As a guest of the Australian Shukokai Karate Association (A.S.K.A.), I had been invited over to interview Kimura sensei and write about his visit. When we met I could scarcely believe my eyes, because he seemed not to have changed at all during the intervening years. We talked for only a short while before his duties required him to change into his karate-gi and begin teaching the small group of yudansha (Dan grades).

This group consisted of Australian instructors. Kimura sensei was running a special training course for them, over four mornings. In the afternoons and evenings he was teaching the general main body of students. To my surprise, and delight, I was invited to join in both courses. I was to learn later that this was a signal honour accorded to no one else prior to myself. As a rule only people belonging to his particular group were permitted to take part in Kimura sensei's courses.

Excited and filled with anticipation, I found it was a case of deja vu, for there I was again, in the third row from the front. As before, the approach was different from my usual karate training experiences. Kimura sensei began the lesson with the words, "With this training I want to make your brains sweat, not your bodies."

I wasn't too sure what he meant by this, but as the lesson progressed it became clearer. Instead of the usual kata (forms), bunkai (application of techniques found in the forms relating to combat) and combination training, he concentrated for the first lesson on gyaku-zuki (reverse punch). For over two hours we looked at, dissected and executed this most primary of karate techniques. On the face of it one might have asked, what is there to look at for two hours. But as Kimura sensei pointed out, "To do karate well you must first of all know your body well". So with this in mind, it was not only our arms and fists that did the punching, but our entire bodies. As the days moved on the instructor group worked hard to take on board the information their sensei was imparting, and by day four most them could 'feel' a difference in their punching techniques.

"Maeken-zuki (leading hand punch) and gyaku-zuki should flow from each other naturally," Kimura sensei said. He told us that he felt people stand too close when engaged in kumite (free fighting). I saw him demonstrate how it was possible to be out of reach of an opponent

Kimura sensei with Author in Melbourne, Australia.

one second, and 'on top of him' the next. He showed this many times during the course.

Although this training was enjoyable, the highlight of my trip were the opportunities I had to sit down with him and talk about his life and his feelings for karate-do. On the occasions that I spoke with him I found him to be a most amicable man. When we had met years previously, when I was a lowly 3rd Kyu, he had taken time after training to talk to me. He was no less forthcoming the second time. He spoke freely in response to my questions, but as I listened it became clear that many of his ideas would be controversial. Nevertheless I found him to be a very traditional Japanese sensei. He did not talk in flowery terms about Zen, or about one's inner self. The message he gave to his students was, "One hit, one kill".

Though I had known of him almost since the inception of my karate career, my knowledge of him as a person was almost nil. So when we sat down in a quiet corner of one of Melbourne's many Japanese restaurants I began by asking him about his youth, and how he came to train in karate in the first place. He told me that for as long as he could remember he had been interested in martial arts. Like every other Japanese child, he had been introduced to them at school.

He was born in the city of Kobe in 1941, but it was not until he was sixteen years old that he first walked into a karate dojo and asked for lessons. His teacher on that first day, and for the rest of his life, was Master Chojiro Tani, headmaster of the Shukokai Karate Association and founder of Tani-ha Shito-ryu. Master Tani had been a long time student of Shito-ryu's founder, Master Kenwa Mabuni, and had started his own branch of this style in 1948 with the blessings of his teacher. This latter is a noteworthy and important factor.

In those early days of training, students concentrated mainly on kihon or basic techniques and kata. Fighting was practiced, but not nearly as much as these two aspects. Although the young Kimura wanted to do more of the type of training which he liked, he was very much a junior in the dojo and so he had to 'do as he was told'. The fighting training which he did was exclusively ippon

Kimura sensei teaching in Europe, around 1969.
Photo - S.W.K.U.

kumite (one attack sparring). However, from time to time he would also train in bunkai from various kata.

As time went by his skill increased. He began to train in both nihon and sanbon kumite (two and three step/technique sparring. Whereas ippon kumite was related to the kata, the freestyle ippon kumite was closer to all out free fighting. He recalled that he had spent a lot of time checking his techniques, not only to simply ensure correct execution but to build up power. Surprisingly, he did not execute his punches on the makiwara (straw bound punching post) used in karate for developing punching ability. Instead he liked to have a friend roll up a gi or karate jacket to form a pad held against the chest, and use that as a target. As he told me, "I found this a much better way than hitting a makiwara, because of the 'live' feedback I got from my friends".

With three of four years of karate training behind him he thought it was about time he entered a few tournaments.The first was the Western Japan Championships. This proved to be a rather inauspicious debut, and on his second attempt a few months later he ended up being disqualified. All this he put down to his inexperience and the fact that the thought of everyone looking on made him very nervous. As a result he was hitting people too hard. As time went by his fortunes changed and success began to come his way. As well as winning tournaments organised by the Rengokai, Kimura sensei eventually became the All Japan Shukokai Champion. He qualified this fact in a typically self effacing way by saying that the standard was not as high that year as it had previously been. I doubt that this was really true, but I was not about to dispute this with him!

His time in competition was short lived. At the age of twenty-four he was sent overseas to teach. His first tour took him to Europe and South Africa, and although still not free from his nervousness, he was

more than happy to go. Looking back he recalled how good it was to meet people from many other countries. That was in 1964, and by 1969 he was on his way back to Europe for the second time. The main reason for this trip was to help one of his seniors from Japan, Nambu sensei, at his dojo in Paris, France. During this same period he found time to visit some of the countries he had gone to during his first trip. He was able to travel to England for the first time, and his arrival caused quite a stir in English karate circles. Students from different styles came to train with him. One result of this visit was the formation of a new Shukokai association in England.

When I asked Kimura sensei how it happened that he went to America, he replied, "I had always had a wish to go to America but I did not know anyone over there, so I had no contacts. Anyway, one day I simply decided to go. I bought a round trip ticket and set off for New York. When I arrived at JFK airport I had no idea where to go, so I jumped into a taxi and asked the driver to take me to Manhattan. I just knew the name from the movies, but I didn't know where it was or what was there, or even what it might be like."

"As we approached the down-town area, I could see all the tall buildings and the heavy traffic, and I began to get a little scared. The driver asked me where in Manhattan I wanted to go. I told him I didn't know anyone and asked to be taken to a hotel that was not too cheap or too expensive."

"So there I was sitting in a hotel room at last, in the middle of New York. I wasn't interested in sightseeing. I wanted to have a look at the New York karate. I looked in the phone book and found a number of dojo. I spoke to a guy and asked him if I could come over and watch. This was okay by him, he said, and so after he had given me directions to find his place I set off. When I got there the people sensed that I was a karate instructor. I sat down with them and we talked about karate. They were very nice to me, and asked me what I wanted to do in America. I explained that I wanted to travel all over the United States. They said that they had friends in such and such a place, so why not go and visit them for a while. I did just this, and at each dojo I visited the people there told me of somewhere else to go. This is how I got to travel around. I was doing really well until I reached Las Vegas. I lost all my money there! After that I returned to the New York area."

"Around that time I had the good fortune to meet a judo man called Mr. Kidachi. He had a dojo and when we became good friends I began to teach karate there. This is how Shukokai karate came to

Kimura sensei teaching in Australia.

the United States. After about two years of teaching at the judo dojo I decided to open up my own dojo, and this I did. It was only small, and for the first three years I lived in it. My bedroom was in the basement and I remember it was full of cockroaches and stuff. This was in Hackensack, New Jersey."

"Now, twenty years later, my house is attached to the dojo. I have two more houses in the same block of land for visiting students to live in. As I said, this has taken twenty years to build up, and all from a financial base of only two hundred dollars."

I asked Kimura sensei about the way his karate was received in Europe and America. He told me that he had convinced people of his karate's effectiveness by asking them to hold a punching pad. Once they had felt the shock through the pad he would ask them if they would like to be able to punch like that. Most said yes. Up until his untimely death on July 7th, 1995, from a massive heart attack, Kimura sensei had built up a student following in many countries around the world.

Touching on the philosophy of karate he said this: "When you are training for a strong technique you are actually developing your body; you are getting an understanding of it. You then begin to 'search' your body and find out about your muscles and how they work. You also have to look at the things in detail and be scientific in your approach. This in turn promotes a sort of philosophy as well. You develop a quality in your techniques, and as you do this you also develop a kind of moral code. If I come across a person who has a good philosophy, but not a strong technique, then I question his or her philosophy. A strong technique makes a good philosophy; it's very easy to understand."

Our conversation then turned to the subject of kata. I had yet to see him teach a kata, though I'm sure he did. Come to think of it, I had yet to see even a photograph of him doing one, but I knew him to be a traditionalist, and so I figured his kata must be there somewhere... He told me he wanted to do 'good' kata, but said it in a way that lead one to believe that he had yet to accomplish this ambition. In his younger days he had never entered the kata events which made up the other half of the tournaments he entered. Although he did say that he liked to watch people performing kata. If it came to a choice between the Itosu and Higaonna style kata, he preferred the Higaonna school.

He saw kata as a tool that one should use to help grasp a better feel-

ing for one's techniques. He was at pains to point out that the punches and blocks must be real.

"In kata," he explained, " we do many types of blocking such as shuto (knife hand), gedan (lower level), jodan (upper level) and so on, so yes, we all know these blocks, but I say, can they really stop a punch? You see, to put life into your kata your have to know how to do the techniques well. There is a big difference between showing a blocking technique, and blocking an actual punch. There are many ways to do a blocks but they should not all be of the 'bang' type. That way you get hurt too. If you know how to block and you are confident so that when you are in a fighting situation you can really do the techniques, then you have something. But you have to make sure that your movements have 'life'."

"If you want to understand the 'art' of karate then your techniques must be like that.   If you don't deliver them like that then you have dancing, and I would not like people to think of karate just as dancing. I want to do some good kata one day, and I'm working on it. When I do do kata, I don't just do it for the sake of it you know. I have some reason for it. I want to give a good impression. It is like an artist when he paints tigers. Sometimes you look at such a painting and think that it is good. It really looks like a tiger. But some artists can paint a tiger that looks like it is coming off the page right at you. That is what I want to do with my kata.   It should not just represent moves, but look 'alive'. That is what I want, but I am still working on it."

"Many people treat kata as if they were a collection. They want more and more kata. I say to people like this, 'Who made up this kata anyway? What were their reasons?' Someone made them up a long time ago. But I could make up a kata too. I often ask myself, why is this movement or that movement so important? Most moves in kata are very good, but not all of them. To be honest, I think one should make

up one's own kata anyway. I'm not talking about people doing this from the beginning, but after a certain level is reached, and you have developed your own feeling. Why do we have to follow a man who made up something three hundred years ago? It's a different world now, a different environment. I'm not being disrespectful here, not at all; this is what people have always done."

You see, my basic karate technique is exactly the same as the technique in my kata and my kumite. There is no difference in that respect. So, if one has good basics one can definitely improve on sparring and kata. By training how to punch right, with just one punch like gyaku-zuki (reverse punch done by the right hand for instance if the left leg is in front) I am learning to master my body. I am understanding things like which muscles work for this punch, and how I have to coordinate my body and so on. From this kind of thinking I can automatically block better, kick better and even move better in an all round way. Given this ability, it is possible to do good kata and good kumite."

I wanted to know what Kimura sensei thought the purpose of training in karate was, apart from the obvious stock answers. Why should people bother to train at all? Thugs are just as likely these days to have a gun or other lethal weapon if they rob you, so what good would karate be then? And in this world of political correctness and leniency towards the criminal, even if a person did defend himself effectively and take a weapon from an attacker, the would-be victim might find himself charged with a more serious offence than the initial perpetrator. So why bother with karate for self defence for instance? This was Kimura sensei's reply.

"But what would happen if you were walking along with your daughter or wife and someone attempted to rape them? You are going to kill that guy aren't you? In such a situation you would have to use your karate. Yes? This is why you have to make sure that it works. That it really works. Although this is not the main goal of karate training it is a major one."

"In the book 'Hagakure' there is a good point made about this whole subject. The samurai were advised in olden days never to use their swords, but that if they had to use them they should be sure that the techniques worked. It is the same for karate I think. The sword had to be sharp, strong and effective. Similarly your karate techniques have to be sharp and strong. But I believe that there are a lot of things necessary to reach that level of karate effectiveness. It takes a lot of time, effort and concentration. But this is what traditional karate is all about. First we learn karate-jutsu and then through this comes karate-do. From strong training we develop a way of life."

"Training in karate, or any martial art for that matter, also brings other benefits. By training you are very simply achieving something. for instance, I always set a goal and than try to achieve it. Just like in business in fact. If you set up in business you start by saying to yourself that you want to have this kind of business or that kind of business. You formulate your goals and go for it. I do this myself. I am a karate man. I say to myself that I want this kind of technique. Then I work hard to get it. After a while I achieve it and feel good about myself. But I don't forget how I got into this position. Once I have reached my goal I become confident in my ability. This is what makes success. But this feeling does not last forever, so I then set a higher goal and start over again. By doing this within the karate field I am able to do the same thing in my life. Then just as in karate my success gives me confidence to do more."

"This is the type of value and purpose of training today, not just for fighting. This refers to what I was saying about philosophy; that it comes from your technique. It comes through your technique.

Another value for me has been the opportunities that karate has given for travel and for meeting a great many people. I have learned things which I could not have learned in any other way. I have experienced other cultures from travel as well."

Since Kimura sensei had been training for many years, I wanted to know how his training had changed, if at all, during that period. In reply, he said, "When you are young, then your spirit is the most important thing. Technically your karate should be o.k. but it is your spirit that should be foremost at that time. You must be willing to sweat, to be devoted. Personally, I have felt differently during each decade of my life so far. For older people I feel it is more important to make sure that they are doing the techniques as correctly as possible. Also you should take care of your body and make sure that you are warmed up correctly. This is why you need a good teacher, so that you know that the things which you are doing are right."

So I asked him what makes a good teacher.

"To become a good leader, and after all that it is what a teacher is, you must first be wise. As well as wise you should also be considerate. And finally, you must have courage. If a person has these qualities then you have leadership and such a person will be a good teacher."

Towards the end of my final interview with Kimura sensei I asked him a question unlike any I usually ask. How would he like to be remembered? I did this with the mistaken certainty that he would be around for many years to come.

"The way I see it," he began, "is that my dojo belongs to all my students. It is their Shukokai hombu (headquarters). After I die, say in fifteen to twenty years maybe?...I will leave half my things to my wife

and family, and half to my students. I would like something to go back to all the countries that have supported me all this time. So that would include funds to help set up a dojo in each country that does not have one at present. That way, students will have somewhere they can go and train in their style of karate. Also, I will be leaving something worthwhile for the next generation, not just a memory. Around the world there are many people who are motivated but who do not have a dojo they can afford to get to. This way, they will have, and once they know the techniques well they can pass them on to yet another generation."

I remember thinking at that time what a great idea this was, and how fortunate the students were to have a sensei who thought in this way.

Less than four years after this conversation with him, Kimura sensei was dead. Some time during the evening of Friday, 7th July 1995, while relaxing at home, he suffered a massive heart attack. He was fifty-four years old. I count myself lucky to have met him and to have had the opportunity to train with him. I will remember him not only for his powerful techniques and the graceful way in which he did them, but also for his down-to-earth, friendly attitude towards me.

Rest in peace, sensei.

Still Finding Something New
Seiichi Sugano's Forty Year Aikido Odyssey

You are standing outside the dojo of Master Morihei Ueshiba's aikido dojo. You are just fifteen years old, and you are about to ask if you can become an apprentice in the art produced by the great man. This happened to Sugano sensei. It was the beginning of a journey that has lasted over forty years.

Born in Hokkaido, Japan's most northern island, he travelled down to Tokyo to complete his education. On his arrival he enrolled at the Kodokan, home of judo, and for the next three years he could be found more often on the mats than behind a book. During this time he read about aikido and its founder O-Sensei Ueshiba. One day he decided to go directly to the aikido hombu and ask for instruction. He was accepted as an uchi-deshi or inside student. From that point he moved into the dojo and began training every day. This was not the usual way to become a disciple, but with the help of a senior instructor at the hombu, his introduction to the 'way of peace' began.

His training started at 6.30 a.m. each day. Even before he had time to think of aikido though, he and the other uchi-deshi had to clean the dojo. Six classes per day were the backbone of the uchi-deshi's schedule, and they were expected to do extra training throughout the day as well as to accompany Ueshiba sensei or any of the other senior instructors who were teaching outside the hombu. When I interviewed Sugano sensei I asked him what this training had been like, way back then. He told me that he could remember little in detail, but one thing had stuck permanently in his mind: how hungry he always was.

"I was always hungry. There was so much training every day and I was very keen. I never had a plan to get a senior grade, or to become

Seilchi Sugano (at left, front row) was privileged to be one of the young apprentices trained by Master Morihei Ueshiba (standing), the founder of modern aikido.

Photograph courtesy of Australasian Fighting Arts magazine.

a teacher. I was just interested in training. Although it was very hard at times, I was never frightened or worried by that. We never received any secret information or anything like that, but we were involved with aikido twenty-four hours a day and so eventually we developed much more attentiveness to what we were doing than the average student. Quite often people think that we had some kind of special training or something like that, but this is not how it was. We just had so much involvement, all day, that we took in O-sensei's teaching that much better. If you compare the amount of time we

spent in his company, and in training with him and compare it with the amount of time for a normal student who came to the dojo only a few times a week, it is simple to see why we were in fact different."

Sugano sensei was quick to dispel any thoughts of O-Sensei having any supernatural powers. "I don't believe he had anything like that. He was a very spiritual man, very religious. So maybe his lifestyle and the fact that he had a connection with another religious group made some people think like that. He was a man, so I don't credit he could do some of the things that other people have said he was capable of. I don't for instance believe he could vaporize and then appear in another place. He did not teach such things. I was young then and I had more than enough to think about just being attentive to him. As far as I know, none of the uchi-deshi thought of him in that

Sugano sensei using a boken (wooden sword)

Photograph - author

way. One thing I do remember though was his ability to know what was going on elsewhere in the dojo or his home. Even though he was not in the dojo or at home, he seemed to know."

I wanted to ask if Sugano sensei had registered any changes in aikido over the forty years in which he had been training. "Yes," he said, "this is only natural. Before the Second World War the training was much rougher than at present. By this I mean that aikido is much more stylised today. This is due to aikido's exposure to many people during those years. And also, people understand their bodies and the world around them much more in a certain sense. Things have changed a great deal. You see, before aikido spread out into the present situation, everyone who was involved with it were to varying degrees directly connected to O-Sensei. That meant a relatively small number of individuals whose exposure to other things would not have been so great as it now is."

"From my personal standpoint too, my own aikido has also changed as I have grown older and spent many years of training. My understanding has evolved and my aikido has developed. Other teachers will be teaching maybe in a different way, according to the way they are thinking and the different experiences which they have had."

"It's not that you change things in the sense that you plan such changes to happen at various points, or when you reach a certain age. O-Sensei said that up to the age of twenty-five you are more fitted for hard training. You can concentrate on the physical techniques at that time and train hard because you are still growing and getting stronger. By the time you are thirty you should be expanding your technical understanding based on experience as well as purely on your physical ability. By this time you have stopped growing physically anyway, but your aikido has not stopped. So your aikido changes without a plan; in a sense it evolves without your knowing exactly how."

"Of course I am speaking generally here, and about people who began training when they are young and then continue. And again, the way you evolve also has a lot to do with who your teacher is, whose teachings you are following; this will make a lot of difference to your development. My own technical understanding is very different now from what it was twenty years ago and even ten years ago. As experience grows with time, and someone looks at my technique and believes they can see no change, this does not mean that I have not changed on the inside. You see, now I have a better understanding of the techniques, or what I am doing, so things have changed, even though to an onlooker this may not be obvious."

"In connection with my teaching, I don't like to direct people. So one of my students in Europe said that my way of teaching was more difficult to follow than that of other teachers. Not that I do things which are more difficult to do than the things which other teachers do. It is in the way I teach. He said that I was difficult to copy. That some of the more stylised teachers were easier to follow for the students. They could imitate the physical form more easily. With the way I teach such things are a little more difficult, because, as I said, I don't like to direct people."

"When I am teaching I like to give up the information side and try to get people to move spontaneously. You know, even on the same day my movements might be quite different from one class to another. If you look at a teacher who has a strong style, most of their followers have the same style. With me this has not happened as I don't have such a thing. As I said before, my understanding has changed a lot from ten or twenty years ago, so my aikido has also changed along with my better understanding."

"I believe this is what O-sensei meant when he said nothing in aikido is fixed. He gave us a big question mark with aikido. Because

Sugano sensei
demonstrating
a throwing
technique on a
pupil.

Photographs
- author

it is never fixed it therefore works depending on how the individual studies it and pursues its message. This is why we now have many different styles of aikido today. There are so many teachers now. Some say, 'O-sensei did this technique this way, or that way, so now we must all do it the same.' I don't think this is what O-sensei had in mind for aikido. He used to explain his ideas through his own personal religious concepts. Therefore, if someone also made a study of his religion then it might be easier to understand his aikido concepts. To get your ideas over to others you have to use words to convey your feelings. He used his religion to convey his feelings, but he never said we had to follow his religion. He had attained a certain mental state, he had his religious beliefs, and how he felt, and this all appeared in how he approached aikido. On the other hand, Kano sensei used scientific terminology to explain his ideas about judo. The laws of leverage and so on were well known to most people, so this was a good way for them to understand what he was thinking."

"O-sensei's difficulty was that no one understood the language he was using. What I mean by that is that no one understood his basic ideas. If you don't have such a tool as a common language, then you don't say anything, you can't say anything clearly, you just do it. This is why there should not be too much effort put into trying to explain things verbally."

Traditionally the way for a person to learn was for him or her to observe. This trained a student's powers of observation, of course, and created a situation for the master to teach each individual in a different way according to his or her powers of observation, coupled with their understanding. If a master thought that he could formulate the information, then he might give you an explanation of some kind, or some more information. For example, O-sensei's idea of standing or posture was related to a human being standing between heaven and earth. Now if this concept drew a response from you, it follows that you would not hunch your back or hold your body in a bad posture. This is the kind of thing he would talk about."

"It is not necessary to give explanations all the time, you see. In my own case, in much of the teaching I do, I do try to give students an explanation, piece by piece. I try to pick the right moment when I think the student will understand what I'm about to say. It is no good if I just tell a student something, but their understanding of aikido is not deep enough to take in what I mean. After a while, I suppose we all come up with some ways of describing the physical form of a technique. But this is hardly the whole of aikido. O-sensei himself said that teachers can only impart a fraction of the technique. He believed that each student had to make his or her own efforts to understand and thus bring aikido to life, again. This is why we need to study what aikido is."

In his early days at the hombu dojo, Sugano sensei and the other uchi-deshi used many different training methods in order to increase their ability and understanding. I asked him what type of extra curricula activity they engaged in.

"We trained with the bokken (wooden swords) and we also went running. Sometimes we would train with throwing knives (shuriken) and even go to demonstrations of other martial arts to see how they moved and what techniques they employed. As the training of the university dojos was usually a bit tougher than at the hombu, we would go and visit them too. Back then there was a makiwara (punching board used in karate-do) just outside the hombu, and quite often we would use it to work on our atemi (striking) techniques. I don't know if it helped me particularly or not, but in those days I was young and so I would try many different things. As the makiwara was just outside the dojo I used it."

"O-sensei never told us to do any of this, we just did it. As far as the makiwara is concerned, I feel that in order to have effective atemi you need to at last know how to make a proper fist. Otherwise you hurt yourself. You know, I am asked many times about atemi in aikido. It would be very easy to say, yes, I can use atemi here or at this point I can kick. But unless you train properly, those techniques will not be effective. So if this is what you want from your aikido then you have to train in this way. Generally though this kind of attention to atemi is not necessary. In the case of the aikido which I teach, atemi is used for reasons other than just finishing off an opponent. I use it to give a sense of the right direction, the right distance and also to prevent a second attack. This is how I see atemi. In my aikido I am trying to attain one continuous movement and atemi is a part of that movement. It is not a separate thing that is added on to a technique at this

Sugano
sensei
shows
a throwing
technique
from a
kneeling
position.

Photos-
author

place or that point. it is an essential part of the overall movement, and if you are not moving correctly you will find that you cannot use atemi properly."

I had heard that the aikido people had engaged in an 'exchange of techniques' with students of Nippon Kenpo, and I was keen to discover the outcome of the meeting. Sugano sensei said, "It was not what you are thinking I'm sure. In my early days I had a friend whose friend was training in Nippon Kenpo. So one day we went along to watch it and we ended up having an informal exchange. They had some very interesting techniques, kicking and punching. Also they had some jujutsu type techniques that were effective, but the style was not developed to use against aikido. We had to watch out for the distances between us. This was one of the main points and differ-

ences, but it was a good experiment for all of us I think."

"As well as this kind of extra training on top of our normal training, we would also take part in special camps. These usually lasted for ten days and the training there would include running, push-ups and other exercises in addition to the long days of actual aikido work."
I asked Sugano sensei if these camps covered training in Misogi or purification rituals. I raised this matter because I knew that Ueshiba sensei used such methods himself.

"Misogi is a Shinto term. It relates to a person purifying the body and mind. There are many different ways of doing this. Normally in traditional aikido training we use some methods at the start of practise. We do this without explanation and it is symbolic of what we are about to do. That is, we want to clear our bodies to receive energy. According to O-sensei, the whole of aikido is a kind of Misogi. His idea was that you should purify your body and mind in order to receive the universal energy. This is comparable to what is done in Shinto, where you always purify yourself before receiving whatever comes into your body."

Life for an uchi-deshi was without doubt difficult, and given that they all lived and trained under such a regime, it is no wonder that Sugano sensei's fellow students moved on to become teachers of aikido who are now known and respected around the world.

"There were deshi who were senior to me. These were people who had started training before me. Mr. Tamura now lives in France. Mr. Yamada is in New York. Mr. Chiba, who spent many years living in England, now lives in San Diego, California. Mr. Kanai lives in Boston and I live in New York. I'm not sure how it was that all of us came to leave Japan after we had completed our uchi-deshi training. There were no problems at the hombu or anything like that. The real rea-

Sugano sensei in a reflective mood - Photograph - author.

son probably is that aikido started to expand worldwide just then, and we as a group were receiving invitations to go abroad."

"For example at that time I was married to an Australian woman. I didn't have a plan to move to Australia to teach aikido. My then wife and I came here so that I could meet my new family. So, you see, within a three year period between 1964 and 1967 all the uchi-deshi had left Japan and moved abroad. So as I said, there was no master plan, things just happened that way. I think that we were the last group to go through the uchi-deshi type of training and then go overseas. These days, people are more likely to become teachers at the hombu dojo. They have to live at the dojo for only one year, and also they have to be college graduates. So things have changed a little from my time."

Before our conversation came to an end, I wanted to hear Sugano sensei's recollections and thoughts on a number of things which have been said about or attributed to O-sensei Ueshiba. In replying, Sugano sensei was very cautious at first.

"We have to be very careful here," he began. "This is because sometimes things get confused in translation. A word is changed here and another word there, and a quote takes on a whole new meaning. Because of the way O-sensei spoke, even Japanese people had, and still have, trouble in understanding exactly what he was saying. The Japanese language is far more abstract than the English. So it is very difficult to translate abstract ideas into exact words with exact meanings. Many of O-sensei's teachings do not have strong conclusions."

I took this in and then continued questioning along the same lines, in the hope that Sugano sensei's ideas on the thoughts of his teacher would shed light where previously there had been little. That he would offer insights into a man who would remain for most of us a constant enigma. I asked why O-sensei often referred to aikido as 'the Way of Peace'.

"He attained a very high mental state through his religion. He was always thinking about peace, so obviously he expressed ideas that the ultimate way of training in aikido was to try to achieve, or create, world peace. The aims may seem contradictory at first because aikido is generally regarded as primarily a martial art. Yet, O-sensei spoke of aikido as a way of peace, and I think therefore that he intended that his followers should be spreading peace. He told us that such ideas were the ideal, and that to dwell only on the martial aspects of aikido was a false pursuit. He said that we should try to show this feeling of peace in our own training. You see most people think only of the physical side, and even if you are watching others training, you are seeing only the physical side, but if you are only thinking of the self defence aspect or being strong, then your training will not lead to peace. But first, we have to find this peace inside ourselves."

Another expression I wanted to ask about was 'Mu'. It usually translated as 'nothingness', and I had read somewhere that O-sensei taught that to understand aikido one had to 'link oneself to true emptiness'. In this connection Sugano sensei said:

"Even the idea of nothingness is still a form of attachment, I believe. So if you go about thinking of nothingness, you are attached to it. It becomes an aspiration. I think O-sensei's idea of emptiness was to adopt a frame of mind that left you open to being receptive to everything. If you have a set idea about what something is then you can't receive a new concept or make new discoveries. This is the same with peace. If two people are already full of their own ideas, and these ideas are different, then it is difficult for them to accept the other person's point of view.. The result is... no peace."

I continued my interview by asking about some more words attributed to O-sensei:

"The art of peace has no set form. Ultimately you must also forget about technique. The further you progress the fewer teachings there are. The great path is really no path."

Sugano sensei replied. "Well... if he said exactly that, I think he was probably talking again about being open minded, don't you think? Not fixing your mind on one thing. For instance on the physical side of training, the aikido technique is not a precise movement. Each time you do what is ostensibly the same technique it is not exactly the same, is it? I think O-sensei was trying to get people to grasp this

idea and not become attached to one form, or one way of doing something."

"You see, O-sensei's teaching method was not like many might think of as teaching. He would simply walk into the dojo and demonstrate his ideas. Sometimes he would talk a little about things, but never as a regular thing and certainly not all the time. I remember one day I was in the office at the hombu and O-sensei came in. He asked me if I knew how to use weapons. Of course I said that I didn't. So right then he took me into the dojo and showed me what to do. This is an example of how he used to teach. I know he did the same thing with other people too. He would first demonstrate what he wanted you to do, and then you had to work at it until you found something. In the old days I think this was the way that all martial arts were taught. I don't think that any of the old masters had the concept of a syllabus or gradings. They would just show things and the students would follow."

"Today I think we have to teach in a way that helps people to see what O-sensei was trying to achieve. He was pursuing something. Therefore we students should follow the master's desire to pursue knowledge, not just to master the techniques. This being so, I can't see any usefulness in saying that O-sensei used to do a particular technique this way or that way, at that point in time, and that therefore we in turn must always do it in the same way. I don't think that this is following the master."

"He never fixed anything this way himself. He was searching for something and following his ideas. We should continue to search for that same thing he spent his life looking for. For me, my obligation to O-sensei is to follow the development he made and then try to find the things I'm looking for in aikido. First you try to follow the teacher, but it is wrong if the teacher makes all the students do something in a particular way and tells them they are wrong if the can't do it. As a teacher I am trying to help a person discover and develop feelings from within themselves."

Even though Sugano sensei has over forty years of aikido training behind him, he told me he was still finding something new. He continues to find the whole idea of aikido fascinating.

"It's like one big question mark," he said. "O-sensei knew that it is important to keep looking."

I asked him if he thought he would recognise what it was he was searching for should he ever come across it. "Probably not," he replied, "but that's the fascinating part of aikido. That's the difficult part. If anything were fixed, then once I had found it and then mastered it, it would be over. With aikido I am searching for some idea, a feeling if you like, and just when I think I have found something I realise there is more and I have to continue. Some people fix their idea of aikido, but I think these people have stopped. Even if you become too old or infirm, or have some type of injury and have to stop training in the techniques of aikido, you do not have to stop at that point. Aikido is boundless. It is a way of seeing life."

The Essential Okinawan
The Life and Times of Shoshin Nagamine

Shoshin Nagamine sensei was among the most senior karateka in the world. It was not his rank of judan (tenth Dan) that made him so, for there are a handful of other men who hold such a degree of excellence, and many more who are, shall we say, pretenders to such an achievement. Rather it was his age and the extraordinary length of time he was involved with his beloved art of karate-do. For seventy years he turned towards the shomen (main wall of the dojo), bowed and began training.

Born in Tomari-son, Naha, the capital of Okinawa on July 15th, 1907, he was rather small at birth and remained somewhat undersized through his childhood. His father Shoho and his mother Gozei did not worry too much about him though, as he was just as wild as any other boy of his age. He entered high school in 1923 but shortly afterwards fell ill. The medication he was given proved useless and so he resorted to diet and exercise to improve his health. The exercise chosen was karate. His neighbour, Mr. Chojin Kuba, taught karate in his backyard and it was here that the young Nagamine first received his instruction, in 1925.

Time passed and he grew stronger from his daily workouts. By the time he was twenty he felt stronger than he had ever felt before. In his senior year he was captain of the karate team, and took part in the annual martial arts competition held between the various schools from around the island. It was during this period that he began to take training very seriously indeed, working at his karate every night in the grounds of the Tomari primary school under the watchful eye of an old master by the name of Kotatsu Iha.

Once he had graduated, his desire to train harder increased, and to this end he began to make the eight kilometer walk to Shuri each evening to train under Taro Shimabukuro sensei. Although Shimabukuro was only one year older than Nagamine sensei, the latter felt that the long walks were worth it so that he could learn more. Indeed Nagamine sensei was full of praise for his youthful teacher, saying that it was he who fired his dreams of mastering karate. So steeped in his training did he become that it was said his appetite for karate was greater than his appetite for food.

For a short time he also trained under Ankichi Arakaki sensei, who is now known to every serious student of karate history as a brilliant karate-ka who died tragically at the age of twenty-eight from complications due to ulcers. In 1928 at the age of twenty-one Nagamine sensei was conscripted into the Japanese army. In April the same year he saw action in Sainan, China. The rest of his national service proved less eventful and once more he found himself home in Okinawa. Having received an honourable discharge he looked around for some way to make a living, and like other conscripts he joined the police. He continued to train in karate as often as his police duties would allow, and met the famous master Chotoku Kyan, whose pupil he became. In April 1936 he was sent to Tokyo for six months training with the metropolitan police. While he was there he received teaching from yet another notable teacher, Choki Motobu sensei, in the Hongo district of the city.

As the years passed he rose through the ranks of both the police force and karate, and in 1940 on the recommendation of Master Chojun Miyagi, the founder of Goju-ryu karate-do, Nagamine sensei was awarded the title of Renshi by the Butokukai (the governing body of martial arts in Japan at the time). He attended a festival of martial arts staged by the Butokukai and was so impressed by what he saw as similarities between karate and kendo (Japanese fencing with

bamboo swords) that he started training in kendo also Eventually he took part in the inter-police contests and was awarded sandan (3rd Dan) rank in 1941. During the second world war he was in charge of rations distribution from his police station in Naha. This put him in a very dangerous position when the battle for Okinawa drew closer. When the American marines landed in 1945, he, along with other members of the police force, became part of the defending army. One June 23rd, 1945, news reached the small band of policemen who were trapped in a bunker that Lieutenant General Mitsuru Ushijima had followed the example set by the Commanding Officers of both the 62nd and 63rd divisions of the Japanese army and committed suicide. At that point, Nagamine sensei realised the futility of fighting on and in company with the other policemen he surrendered.

Although karate was the furthest thing from his mind at this time, fate would step in to keep alive a spark of interest where once there had been a burning desire. While working as a prisoner of war transporting casualties from Iraha village, he came across a book lying in the dirt at the side of the road. Instinctively he stooped down and picked it up. As he cleared away the mud and dirt from the front cover he was amazed to find it was a book by the great karate master Gichin Funakoshi, entitled 'Karate-do Nyumon" or ' Introduction to the Way of Karate'. His reading of the book inspired him and he determined once again to live his life by the way of the fist, and found new strength to face the many hardships that his present situation forced upon him.

By the summer of 1947 he had been allocated a house in the Makishi district of Naha, and shortly afterwards he began to teach karate in a makeshift dojo which he had opened in his backyard. He felt very strongly at this time that the war had stripped his homeland not only of ancient buildings and the landscape terraces of the small farms, but more seriously it had destroyed in the younger generation of

Okinawans a sense of culture. Once known throughout Asia as 'the land of courtesy', Okinawa was now facing a very uncertain future. Most of the buildings had been razed to the ground. In the day to day struggle for survival, many found the battle to stay morally and spiritually intact just too hard.

Nevertheless, Nagamine sensei, together with kindred spirits, did his best to re-introduce the youth of the island to a part of their culture. He believed that in some measure he was helping them to rise above the devastation which surrounded them. In 1951 however he had to face a tragedy which not only shattered him at the time, but filled him with remorse for the rest of his days. At the beginning of that year he was busy training about sixty young men from his police command on the Motobu peninsula. A judo competition was in the offing between a number of police stations around the island. As part of their training, Nagamine sensei's men also did karate. But during one workout a young policeman was accidentally killed. In spite of this, the team went on to win the event.

Shortly afterwards he resigned from the police force and set up home at 3-14-1 Kumoji, Naha, in January 1953. Here he had not only his home but a purpose built dojo. He named it the Kodokan and called his method of karate Matsubayashi Shorin-ryu. Although his dojo was successful, his first few attempts at business were not, and but for the chance reading of two books, he may well have abandoned karate to concentrate on making a living. The first book, 'Teshhukoji no Shinmenboku' told of a master swordsman named Tesshu, and how through his study of Buddhism he found his true self. This work gave Nagamine sensei the encouragement he needed to carry on with his training in karate. The second book was Musashi Miyamoto's 'Go-ri-no-sho' or 'Book of Five Rings', which has had such a tremendous influence on western readers.

The common thread running through both books was how both authors had brought together their physical and spiritual understanding to accomplish their goals. These themes inspired Nagamine sensei greatly. He also saw for the first time the need to have a spiritual element within his karate. From then on he worked to bring together the way of Zen, and the way of the empty hand, karate. Nagamine sensei would meditate for fifteen minutes before each karate training session, as I witnessed for myself. This, he said, strengthened his mind to realise that true victory comes without fighting.

When I met Nagamine sensei in November 1992 he was eighty-five years old and still training every day. His gentle manner, in my opinion the hallmark of a true master of budo, put me at my ease at once. My request for an interview was granted without fuss or pomp of any kind, and I can remember wishing that some of the lesser 'masters' I had met over the years would have taken a leaf out of this man's book.

Our conversation the following evening turned first to the subject of kata. Every traditional school of karate has a number of these at the heart of its practice, so I wondered what thoughts he had on them and would he care to share them with me.

"I believe", he began, "that the kata we practice today is about seventy percent Okinawan and about thirty per cent Chinese in content. We can trace many of these movements back as far as the 16th century, and can see where Okinawan kenpo and Chinese martial arts started to exchange and mix."

"Of course the great contribution that was made to karate by Okinawa was not kata, but the makiwara (a stout post set in the earth and used to condition the hands, particularly the first two knuckles of the fist). In China they had, and still have, many tools to develop techniques, but it was the Okinawans who devised and developed the makiwara that we know today. In olden times men used to gather in backyards all over Okinawa to hit the makiwara. I knew a person who did this even though he never visited a karate dojo."

"Also, when people travelled to China and returned home, they practiced many of their kata with stretched (open) hands as the Chinese did. But when they saw how strongly a fist could be made they changed the kata by making a fist instead. Goju-ryu karate is an example of this. I remember that about seventy years ago, people from that tradition changed the shape of the hands. Uechi ryu karate has also been changed a little from the way it was done in China. But they have kept the old way when training in sanchin kata."

"I want to emphasise that this way or that way is not a question of being better, or worse, but simply different. So I want to stress that the martial arts kata that came from China have been changed and are now more Okinawan."

I knew that Nagamine sensei had know the late karate master Chojun Miyagi, the found of Goju ryu karate-do. As a student of that tradition myself, I asked him to share some of his memories of the famous man.

"I spent about seven or eight years with Miyagi sensei at the Okinawan police academy here in Naha. We became friends, even though he was a lot older than I, and of course he was very much my senior in karate. At the police academy I used to teach the procedure of the law, and Miyagi sensei used to teach karate. It was he who recommended me for the title of 'renshi' (expert teacher) in 1940. He was a very strong person with a pleasant character and his karate was really skilful."

As an Okinawan, Nagamine sensei sees himself as a Ryukyujin or

native of the Ryukyu islands, like many of his generation, and not as a Japanese. I asked him why he thought it was that the Japanese styles of karate seem to have become more popular around the world than those styles practiced in Okinawa, karate's very birthplace.

"Well," he said, "you know for a fact how very smart the Japanese are when it comes to adapting things. In order to make karate more popular they have developed it as a sport, and this has helped to increase the number of people doing karate. They have developed the numbers of people, but in my opinion they have not developed the minds and characters of the majority of these people. So now the quantity is good but not the quality. The main reason for this is that many Japanese karate teachers want to eat from karate. In other words they want to make a living from it, and furthermore they want to be sportsmen and women."

"Admittedly, there is a sporting element in Okinawan karate today, but this is balanced by the culture we have here and our traditional philosophy. We have not dropped the traditional side of things as the Japanese have tended to do. So this makes it less attractive for people who are looking for a sporting pastime. Now, sporting people have changed the kata, and most of them no longer have any meaning. You see it is vital to understand kata as they are at the heart of karate. From understanding your kata will come all the other things. If kata has no real meaning in it, then it is not kata at all, just movements."

"What you have to understand is this. The kata as you do them in the dojo are only the basic principles. It takes a tremendous amount of time and effort to develop your formal kata ability. Now if you train yourself to do this, and you keep in mind other techniques that may not be seen in the kata, for example hooking kicks, punches and so on, then by studying your kata for a long time you will subconsciously develop the skills for combating even unorthodox techniques."

"So the best way is to stick with the old traditional techniques (kata) but always think about how you would use them in application. This has to do with the idea of 'Shu-Ha-Ri' or Obedience-Break Away-Transcend. (First you train exactly as taught, then you experiment and bring your own experience, and then hopefully go beyond this level). When you have a problem you go to your kata and then develop those techniques which will help you solve your problem. This also has to do with your mind, not just the physical techniques. You know about Musashi Miyamoto? Well he used the same way of training; his mind was very strong."

"Then there is the question of communication between people, which is very important. You should always take the opportunity to learn from others and their martial arts. But for things to go smoothly a person must have self confidence. Once this is the case then we can all train together. It doesn't matter what kind of karate you do. Of course your roots are important. That is your heritage after all. But it is more important to be a good person and always behave properly. In both karate and life you must learn to rely on yourself and have confidence. At the same time you should be humble; this too is vital."

"Compare someone who does karate with someone who has in his possession some dynamite. That person can use the dynamite to make a tunnel through a mountain to build something useful like a road, or like a terrorist he can use it to blow people up; karate is just like the dynamite. We have an obligation to try to use it for a good purpose. It should always be useful and constructive. In this connection I would advise people to take up meditation as in Zen, because that is good for everyone."

Towards the end of our conversation I expressed an opinion that

many people seem to drop ideas like 'respect for others' at the door of the dojo as they leave it. Personal integrity seems to disappear for them once they are out of the environmental influences of the dojo. I wondered what he might think, if anything, of my observations.

"To behave as you describe is not the way of karate. I know that for instance a person will train very hard if someone is watching, but then stop as soon as the spectator has gone. In karate you have to train with the same attitude all the time, and it should not matter if people are watching you or not. (A Zen saying is to behave with others as you do when alone, and to behave alone as you would with others).

"In karate we have a principle called Shin-Gi-Tai which means Spirit-Technique-Body. This means that to do karate well and to understand it properly one has to harmonise these three things. Today I think there is an over emphasis on Gi and Tai, Technique and Body, The Shin or Spirit of the person is often left behind while the other two aspects are worked on. Technique and power seem to be the reasons why some people are doing karate today. This is now a much bigger problem than it was some sixty years ago. We should not forget to build a person's spirit and character. This is very important and I want to emphasise it."

"The decline has come about because people want to do karate just for sport or business. To adopt the principles of Shin or Spirit through karate is very hard. To be successful at it takes a long time. People today want things too quickly and it is much easier to train just your body without the discipline of Shin. The ability to do techniques comes from your knowledge and training in those techniques, but your wisdom comes from your mind and heart. It is the fashion to look at karate techniques and try to explain them with scientific information. Everything has to be logical for the modern person to accept how things work. But this leads to them forgetting to look for the 'feeling' of the techniques, and this comes from, if you like, the mind."

"In the end, the ability to make things work comes from your feeling for the techniques of karate. In future I should like to see more attention given to a student's education. If karate is to be understood by people, we must educate them to develop a good feeling."

Nagamine sensei passed away in 1997 at the age of ninety. His death was felt by the whole Okinawan karate community. He was, as well as being a master of karate-do, a lay teacher of Zen, and an author. I consider myself very fortunate to have spent time with him, brief though it was. I am truly grateful for his kindness towards me.

The Fighting Arts of a Holy Dragon
A Meeting with Sifu Tei Seiryu

Tokyo is a city of over twelve million souls, and as one might expect there is no shortage of martial arts nor of people to teach them. It was June 1987 and I was in Japan to further my knowledge of Goju-ryu karate-do. For me this meant a half hour train ride each morning from Ikebukuro station to the outlying district of Kyosei. In truth I was happy to be leaving the city behind each day, and as my schedule took me in the opposite direction to the ebb and flow of the salary men, my time in transit was at least bearable.

It was on one of my rare nights off from the dojo, whilst I was searching for a good place to eat in the narrow streets close to where I was living that I came upon the martial arts school run by Master Tei Seiryu. He was the teaching headmaster of the Chuka Kokujutsu-Kai. On that first night, hunger claimed priority and after looking through the doorway of the school for a few moments I set off again in search of sustenance. I was to return later that week and this time go inside.

I was made very welcome both by the students and by their teacher. Once I was seated at one end of the training area I was served Japanese green tea. With the aid of an interpreter, Miss Hosoo, I had a short first conversation with sifu Seiryu, and this led to an invitation to return the following night when I would be granted an interview about his training and the many arts that are studied and taught within the Chuka Kokujutsu-kai.

In due course I arrived at Master Seiryu's school just before seven the next night. The appointment had been made for seven precisely, and if there was one thing I had learned from my time training in the

Sifu Tei Seiryu
in his Tokyo
school.

Photograph - author

martial arts it was that punctuality was not just appreciated, it was expected. Once again I was offered tea, accepted it and looked around me. The school was already a hive of activity, with students working out in their various arts. Most were in twoes and threes, while others practiced their forms alone. Still others trained in some of the many Chinese weapons from racks which covered the walls.

I had been told the previous evening that the Choku Kokujutsu school of martial arts dated back over two hundred years. It had begun in Beijing (Peking). Within its syllabus one can learn as many as five different kinds of empty hand fighting methods. As sifu Seiryu has knowledge of over fifty types of weapons, the scope for learning this aspect of the art is almost unlimited.

Helped once more by Miss Hosoo, sifu Seiryu explained the various

Sifu Tei Seiryu in on guard posture with traditional halberd and other weapons in the background.

Photograph - author

arts he teaches. Basically they are divided into three Tai Chi systems and two systems which are not related to Tai Chi. Although I had heard of the Chen and Yang styles of Tai Chi, I had not heard of the third, which was called Seiso. Sifu Seiryu said that the Seiso system was from Master Chen Bangrei, the vice-president of the Nangking branch of Kokujutsu in China. It had been adopted by the whole asso-ciation as a 'unifying' form. Within it are the characteristics of both Yang and Chen styles, as well as the martial theory of 'keiiken'. Students who made a study of this art not only did forms but engaged in paired training and did such drills as 'suishu. taida and sanshu'. In addition they trained the single and double edged swords.

The Yang style of Tai Chi taught by sifu Seiryu is the one coming from

Master Yang Cho-ho, a leading figure in modern Tai Chi. In this system also the students train solo and in pairs, and during the latter training do drills known as 'sanshutaida, rensanshu and shuishu'. As well as the single and double edged swords, they also train in the staff, 'kon'.

Chen style is the third Tai Chi style sifu Seiryu teaches. He told me that this is one of the original styles of martial arts known as the 'naika-ken'. Besides the forms known as 'totouken' and 'hozui', students do workouts for actual fighting by focussing on the two person methods of 'sansu' and 'suishu'.

Naiki-ken is the name given by sifu Seiryu to a whole group of martial arts that he said originated in northern China. The two other forms of fighting he teaches also come from the group. Hakkesho is described as one of 'the supreme Chinese martial arts'. When studying this art the student will learn forms of: gaishu-hassho, naishu-roku ju ichi-sho. They will also study the following weapons forms: hakkeken, hakketou, hakke soken, hakkeinyoto and hakkekon-taida. These are the double edged sword, single edged sword, double swords, double knives and the stick, respectively. The students' training is then rounded off by training in the two man form of sanshou.

According to sifu Seiryu, the art of Keiiken, which is also from the Naikaken, is said to be the supreme Chinese martial art. Even so, he says that in comparison with other martial arts it looks plain and simple. For those who become students of this art, the forms which make up the main body of study are: gogyoken, junikeiken, gogyorenkanken, supasui, pashikisui and zoushikisui. In addition the weapons forms found in the Choku Kokujutsukai are included in their work.

Understandably, sifu Seiryu spoke at length and with great enthusi-

asm about all the methods used at the school, and it took about an hour before I could turn the conversation around to him personally. Even when this had begun, he tried on several occasions to steer things away from himself and back on to the martial arts which he was teaching. His humility was clearly genuine, but if I were to have a successful interview I needed to know about his past. Slowly he began to open up on this subject and began by telling me that he had started to learn martial arts at the age of seven, beginning with nin-jutsu. Then age eleven he had switched from the secret arts of his homeland, Japan, to those of China.

"My teacher from that time on was Master Wang. In Japanese his name is Ho Jukin. Sadly he died some time ago and then my training with him came to an end. His training was very hard. I was not naturally gifted with a strong and supple body, so almost all the things we did were difficult for me. Also, in those days I remember that I was never sure exactly what I was doing. You see, the Chinese in those days were very secretive about their martial arts, and consequently they were not very well known in Japan. I just knew that I had to keep going at all costs. I was told that I would have to practice every day if I wanted to learn Kung fu-Chuan fa properly. Now of course, since I have been doing these arts for such a long time, it is part of my life, the way I live."

I asked if there was anything written down about his particular school of martial arts, and if so, how could I set about seeing it. He told me that due to many considerations in the past, nothing was ever put on paper. However, he had recently given interviews and displayed the techniques, at the request of a number of Japanese magazines. In future he said he did intend to record the training methods and produce books.

Sensing the re-appearance of his inclination not to speak about him-

self, I directed my questions towards the subject of his students, and the kind of training they underwent. "First," he replied, "they learn not to fight other people. They do this by becoming stronger than other people. You see in this Chinese martial art school we learn to kill, but also, in the process of learning to kill with physical techniques we learn the mental skills that prevent such a thing happening. Thus we learn how not to kill. In the case of an attack though, we will be able to protect our families and ourselves. Quite apart from the martial aspects of training, this way of life is good for both the physical and mental health of the students. It gives them a strong heart and peace of mind."

"During training I stress stances and correct posture. We do not try to build up big muscles in our arms and legs; we don't try to make strong fists either. What we work for is the capacity to transfer leg power up into our arms and to join that with hand power. So in order to do this, students must be able to make a proper stance;

Sifu Tei Seiryu
showing a version
of Tai Chi's
Single Whip posture.

Photograph - author

one that they need. If they don't do this, then the techniques will be meaningless. We also train to fight in close; closer than western boxing and karate usually do. When we are in close we can use our leg power to punch. If you fight at a bigger distance you need a bigger body and a longer reach. But this is not necessary for us."

"It takes a long time and many hours of hard work to become good at fighting in this way. Even when you are shown how to do a technique, it still needs long hours of work to come to understand it and so be able to use it. The techniques that can kill a man with only a small amount of power are very difficult to master. If you wish to be able to do such things, with one finger for instance, you first have to learn all the vital points on the body. You must also know the correct angle and how much force is used. The timing required when executing such techniques is a further necessity. There are additional techniques for stopping blood flow, and this too needs special understanding and knowledge of timing."

Over the years I had found myself in this position often. There I am sitting opposite a person whom others think of as a teacher, master, sensei or instructor. My tape recorder is taking down everything that is said, and of course the way it is said. Sometimes I have known from the outset that the things I'm being told are untrue. This can be due to a mistaken memory or a downright lie. But can more often be attributed to 'Chinese whispers'.

I had heard so much about the theory of the Death Touch from martial arts people across the spectrum. My overall impression had been that they used it as part of a sales pitch. It did after all promise the prospective student the power of life and death over an adversary. This unrealistic and in my view jaded belief of what the study of martial arts can accomplish would leave the student with little or no real skill, and that much poorer from all the training fees involved. Yet here

was a man who said that he taught such things openly, as part of a larger system, and not as some single deadly art surrounded by mystery and hype. Should I believe him? Certainly such knowledge is out there, somewhere. I do not doubt it. But how many of the people selling it really have this knowledge? From my observations so far, I was inclined to believe that sifu Seiryu did indeed possess such skills; it was not that he was unhappy to display them, but rather that he was not willing to do so. And that is an important distinction.

Training in front of me, as we were speaking, were at least a dozen women. I wondered how, if at all, their training differed from that of the men. I was told that no allowances were made for the gender of students.

"Their training is just the same," was the reply. "Though I have found that in some things women cannot reach the same level as men. This is because of the difference inherent in the physical build of men and women. In general, though there are exceptions, this means that men and women will reach different levels. Also, people differ in their motives for coming to learn here. So not everyone wants to go the whole way. I think it is good that we can offer training to so many people who have different reasons for their attending."

Time was passing, and I could see that sifu Seiryu was repeatedly glancing over at his students with increasing frequency. It was obvious that teaching was uppermost in his mind. I could not let the moment pass however without first trying to return to the man himself. Exercising my patience I managed to achieve this. I learned that he himself trains every day and that he preferred the hakkesho form to anything else. Within it, he claimed, he can hit a single point on a person's body some twelve times in one second.

His personal training also included the cultivation of chi energy. "To

Sifu Tei Seiryu showing a posture with the large curved Chinese sword, sometimes called Big Knife.

Photograph - author

attain chi," he said, "you begin your training by breathing slowly. Then as you get better at it you make your breathing cycles longer and longer until you are taking about five minutes to do one cycle. Next you train yourself to be able to concentrate your consciousness within your hands. Chi travels along the meridians. You must learn to 'inspect' the flow within you so that you can direct it. For instance, you must not allow your chi to flow to your head, as this is very dangerous. I know people who have gone mad by doing this."

I asked him if this type of work was too dangerous for children. "Yes, it is. But I do not teach children. Even our external Kung fu needs concentration of chi and children cannot do this. It is too difficult. So I take children who have reached the age of thirteen or so. This is a good age. Although in some cases there are ten year olds who could begin."

I was able to unearth the fact that weapons use still occupied much of his personal training time. "Yes, weapons are an extension of the hands, therefore I train with them as if they are just another part of my body. In our school we use about fifty different types. Not all at once of course!" Though deadly serious about his art, it was good to see that he had a sense of humour about himself. He disliked any form of weight training and said that push-ups were positively taboo. He maintained that such things only served to stiffen the body. Sit-ups too he said were pointless, since in his school they learn how to build up strong bodies from the inside. He did concede that if students felt that they needed to go running, then this approach was all right by him.

I asked him if he would like to close the interview with some advice for those who might read it later on. This is what he said. "People should work hard at their art, and keep climbing to higher and higher peaks which exist in all martial arts."

With the interview now over, sifu Seiryu left the table and began to mix with his students. He moved to the side of the training area and started to observe the various activities that each group were engaged in. I stayed at the table with Miss Hosoo. As the students became more and more engrossed in their training they would from time to time stop to listen to advice from their teacher. Sifu Seiryu speaks in rather a quiet way and I noticed there were occasions when both teacher and students burst into laughter at some mistake or other. When first I watched the senior students in action, I thought how good they had looked. They seemed to move with real skill and a deep understanding of their art. Still, when it came to training with their teacher the difference between them and sifu Seiryu was very apparent. This could be seen particularly clearly when it came to Pushing Hands. The buzz of effort and concentration continued throughout the evening accompanied by taped music playing quietly

in the background. Slow and almost dreamy, it added an extra dimension to the training.

As I took all this in, I asked Miss Hosoo just exactly what was sifu Seiryu's standing in the Choku Kokujutsukai hierarchy. She told me he was the fourth generation teaching grandmaster, and that the first grandmaster had been a man called Teike Ryukei, whose style was known as Hakke Yoshin Sho. I wondered how a Japanese could have become a teaching grandmaster of a Chinese fighting tradition. So I put this to Miss Hosoo. I was puzzled by her facial reaction to my question. She asked me to wait a moment and went over to where sifu Seiryu was standing. When she came back she sat down at the table and started talking in a low voice. She said that she had asked her teacher whether she could answer my question. Personally I could not see what all the fuss was about my question; it seemed innocuous enough to me. But once she began to tell me the story I understood why she had been concerned and why she had felt the need to ask for permission. What follows is the account she gave to me. I leave it to the reader to weigh the veracity of the tale for himself or herself. I have my own view as to its validity. The story begins in 1979.

In this year, invitations were issued to those people who considered themselves candidates to become the next teaching grandmaster. The invitations came from the Choku Kokujutsukai headquarters in Hong Kong. Along with a number of other senior students from around the world, sifu Seiryu made the trip and once at his destination asked formally to take the required test. For a Japanese to go there at all and seek this promotion must have taken some courage in itself. I turned cold when the details of the required test were related to me. I wondered whether martial arts should exist at all if this was how they had developed. To think of a gentle person such as sifu Seiryu being involved in such savagery was a deep paradox.

In order to become the teaching grandmaster, each applicant was obliged to demonstrate all of the techniques of the system to a board of elder members. The test would end with a display of fighting. Here it was that the test took a unique twist. For not only did the student applicants have to win their fights, but they had to do so even if this resulted in the death of the loser. The people whom they had to fight had been taken off the streets of Hong Kong, years earlier. They had been fed, clothed, housed and trained in deadly fighting techniques. Their lives were dedicated to the day when they would have to be a part of the test. Should they become too old during the wait for the next test, they would be looked after for the rest of their days. Sifu Seiryu almost died in the test.

He fought with five men. Two of them died after the event, and the remaining three, so the story went, were injured so badly that they never walked again. Sifu Seiryu's own injuries were far from slight. He suffered a fractured pelvis and many cuts and abrasions. At the end of the day he was declared the fourth teaching grandmaster to the Teike Ryukei Hakke Yoshin Sho.

Once in office he had begun to open up the teachings to anyone who could make the type of commitment that he himself required. Previously, the school had been open only to members of a select group of families, or those who had intimate ties to them.

My own facial expression had changed during Miss Hosoo's story, and perhaps it was this which made sifu Seiryu come across the dojo floor and back to the table. He affirmed that he had not given permission for the account to be told to me purely to bolster his standing in my eyes, or in the eyes of anyone else who might hear of it. His motive had been to point out to people how potentially dangerous the martial arts could be. The tests are done in great secrecy, and even though he had taken part, he had not been at all happy

with the outcome. On becoming grandmaster he had taken the name he has today. Tei comes from the name of the first grandmaster, and Seiryu translates as 'holy dragon'.

Even though he still carries the legacy of the test in the form of a painful set of hips which are getting worse each year, his fighting techniques have not diminished as far as one can tell. His long black hair, his Chinese clothes, his soft voice and his gentle manner could lead one to believe that he is a holy man. A holy man that is with the whip of a dragon's tail.

Conversations with a Master
The Karate of Hirokazu Kanazawa

I first met Kanazawa sensei in Australia in September 1989. Like most people in the karate world I had heard of him before this. But as I was not a student of the Shotokan style of karate, I never really expected to meet him. When the opportunity arose to actually train with him I jumped at it. Not only that, but I managed to arrange an interview with him the day after the training session.

Since then I have been lucky enough to train with him a number of times in various parts of the world. He has always been very kind to me and treated me as one of his own students. As well as this, he has taken an interest in my karate development and taught me much over the years about the way of the fist, and the ways of the world. As an example I cite here something that happened after a training session with Kanazawa sensei in San Diego, California.

There were several leading teachers taking the training sessions, which covered a three day period. Most of the teachers were gathered around a large circular table. I was walking by, and Kanazawa sensei called me over and had me sit beside him. I felt a little out of my depth, squeezed in between Kanazawa sensei on my right and Ozawa sensei on my left. At that time, Ozawa sensei was the most senior Shotokan teacher in the western world. Unsurprisingly, the conversation turned towards karate, and it was conducted in Japanese. Every now and then Kanazawa sensei would turn and whisper his translation. I would then nod my head as if to show I understood everything he had just said. Neither was fooling the other, so he was not taken in by my assurances. After a time, he turned to me and acknowledging my apprehension in such august company he said, "Don't worry, this is all good experience for you." How right he was, and how kind he was to give me the experience.

Kanazawa sensei with the author - photograph author.

When we met again, it was in London, England, and the next time it was once again in Australia. What follows in this chapter is an amalgam of the conversations I have had with this great karate sensei. In it, he touches on technical points of execution, kata, breathing and the art of Tai Chi, which he has studied for years. This was the first time he had spoken at any length about his experiences with the Chinese art.

Kanazawa sensei performing Kata

(left: author's photograph -
below: Australasian Fighting Arts
magazine photograph)

So first let's look at how Kanazawa sensei felt about kata. As this subject is the keystone of all traditional karate systems, I wanted to know if he had introduced any personal ideas into the way he taught it. He said.

"My kata are till the same as when I learned them when I was younger. Sometimes there might be a small difference in the way something is done, but nothing much. Almost all the timing is the same, but in the kata 'Gangaku' we have a different timing at the point where we stand on one leg and kick yokogeri (side kick). Now, we come out of that move much faster than before. I think this is okay, to be a little different, so this is quite natural. Of course,

every movement must be in the kata, and the rhythm must be the same. As a general rule you should make the stance and technique together, but there are some exceptions here and there. The best way to train in kata is to learn the stances first and be able to move from one to another correctly. After that you can do the techniques that go with the stance. Today I think that most people would become bored if they learned kata this way; but it is the best way."

"You should make a study of your kata, not just memorise them. If you study them you will discover that there are many techniques that are not seen in the usual performance. For example, at the start of 'unsu' kata we make a nekoashidachi (cat stance). Here we can kick as we move forwards but in kata we never do this. Though at the same time in our heads we can think it. Unfortunately there are those who never see beyond the move in the kata, but the mind is very important and we should always be thinking of how we can make things work."

"The movements found in Goju-ryu kata are direct and to the point, but in Shotokan kata the kata often has you doing a block and then turning away in another direction. Such things as this can have four or five different 'meanings' and it is important that people know what they are doing; what the kata is teaching. When Funakoshi sensei (the founder of Shotokan karate) began to teach these kata in Japan, he did so with high school students in mind. I think he wanted to teach the kata more like physical education and it was for this reason that the kata were kept simple."

With the rise of sporting contests in karate kata, I wondered how Kanazawa sensei felt about it. He told me that in his personal opinion he thought that it was okay, and in fact offered an opportunity to display the artistic aspect of karate. This meant that people would put their own feelings into the kata. Also, the rule requiring contestants to start and finish on the same spot meant that they had to work really

hard on their kata, and this he said could only be a good thing. So, what did he stress when he was teaching kata to his students around the world?

"I try to get people to bring their kata to life. For example if spectators are watching you do kata they should see in your movements and expression the fact that the other person, your opponent, is there with you. They should become inspired by what you are doing and it should make sense to them even if they don't know the kata themselves. Of course, on a basic level the students have to get the movements right and get their breathing correct; things like that. But if you can bring it all alive, I think this is the best kata. Then again, it goes without saying you cannot understand kata properly without understanding the bunkai (application of the techniques found in each kata). At kyu grade level I teach only some parts from the kata, but nothing too complicated. The idea is to get the students to look into the kata and see what they are doing. If they just practise the cold movement from the kata then their feeling will not be right."

"I try to get the yudansha (black belt students) to find their own bunkai. They should not wait to be shown everything. They should find out for themselves. Again this means that they have to train in their kata in order to discover the meanings. In the end the kata comes from inside them. Only when this happens will they have very good kata. This is when they will understand that it is not just the exact movement they should master but the principles, the idea. I have seen demonstrations of kata bunkai where the exact moves from the kata are being used, but I do not consider this to be real bunkai."

I asked Kanazawa sensei about attackers with weapons. Would a person have to have at least a working knowledge of the weapon itself in order to be able to counter its use effectively?

Kanazawa sensei showing Tai Chi.

(Fighting Arts International magazine).

"Yes, that's true, and in the kata Bassai Sho for instance we are defending against a bo (staff about six feet or two metres long). So we have to learn to use the bo in order to understand this kata well. In the past this was not such a strange idea after all. For instance kobudo (the art of using weapons) and karate were all the same thing, like two brothers of a single family. At some point though, the two were separated; originally they were the same. But this separation is a relatively new thing."

"Now that we have room at our new hombu dojo in Japan, we also teach kobudo. I teach the bo and nunchaku, and we have a visiting teacher for the jo (four foot staff). In the future we will expand this to all the other weapons found in the study of kobudo. Eventually I would like all our teachers to know how to use the bo, nunchaku, sai and tonfa."

Returning to the subject of empty hand kata, I wanted to ask why Kanazawa sensei was now teaching kata from another tradition, namely Goju-ryu. He told me that there were a number of reasons for this. One he said was because of the use of shikodachi. This stance is a very important one and it is missing from Shotokan karate. He pointed out that it is used by sumo wrestlers and for that reason

alone is worthy of respect. Every student of dan grade level should, in his opinion, learn at least two kata from Goju-ryu and practise them every week.

He himself trains in four of them, namely: seiyunchin, seipai, suparinpei and tensho. I was a little surprised that he did not use the fundamental kata of the system, sanchin. He explained to me that he had once discussed this kata with Mr. Iwai, a man of the same age as Kanazawa sensei who was well known in Japan as a teacher of Goju-ryu. Kanazawa sensei had expressed the view to Mr. Iwai that although sanchin kata was a good kata, he himself had seen students of Goju-ryu straining their bodies and making loud noises in the throat, and so he had a question mark against this. Mr. Iwai had agreed with him and said that doing the kata in this way was wrong. He said that in sanchin kata the hara (centre of the body below the navel) should be strong but not straining. It should be firm.

I then asked if people should make up their own kata. "Yes, maybe," came the response, "but I myself do not feel that I am ready for that yet. I have started to teach a second version of gankaku though. The old version is straight forward and back, but the second version, gankaku-shiho moves in four directions. So now I am teaching twenty-eight kata, not including the four from Goju-ryu."

Anyone who knows Kanazawa sensei will be aware that his skill and knowledge of Shotokan karate is matched by his ability in the Chinese martial art of Tai Chi. It is easy to see that he, along with other notable sensei from the Shotokan tradition, do not move in a rigid manner that so often categorizes this particular style of karate. I wondered why people like himself and Asai sensei of the Japan Karate Association move in a much more relaxed way, teach rounded punching techniques and seem altogether softer than the average Shotokan practitioner. He told me that it had nothing to do with

Film star Lee Marvin watches with obvious admiration as Kanazawa sensei demonstrates a breaking technique. This photograph was probably taken in the early 1960's (?) and comes from Karate & Oriental Arts magazine, no. 7, editor/publisher Paul Crompton. June 1967. (Source: John Chisholme?)

advancing years but with understanding Budo philosophy. He maintained that this was very big and wide, and so a person's technique should be the same. Many think of a single point of focus only, for their technique, but if this is the way you think you will miss out on so much.

"Over thirty years ago, shortly after I returned to Japan from my stay in Hawaii, a very close friend of mine Mr. Yang began to teach me Tai Chi. He and I had been friends for a long time and trained together

at the JKA hombu. His karate was very good and I used to think that he must be doing some other kind of training, something extra. But I didn't know what it was. As he did not volunteer anything I did not ask him. In all that time he never said anything about Tai Chi, just karate. Then one day I heard about a demonstration he had given while I was away in Hawaii. People were talking about it for a long time, so I told him I would like to do Tai Chi."

"It wasn't that I thought Tai Chi was better than karate. You see Mr. Yang was a very nice man; a good person in all parts of his life. Therefore I thought that maybe this comes from Tai Chi. This was my first reason. I know it sounds simple but it genuinely was the cause of my initial interest. Soon after I started I found how difficult it was. It was hard for me because I was used to the severe training of karate. I was still quite young and my understanding of power was all tied in with strength and focus. Mr. Yang would always tell me, 'No, no, do it slowly, you must not use power this way.' His way of making power was to 'move with intention'. I was still thinking too much about my muscles. He would also tell me not to use so much speed, and not to have 'kime' (focus). Also he said to be doing the next movement almost before I had finished the previous one. It got so difficult for me to get any kind of feeling for this type of training that after one year I wanted to give up. I thought that Tai Chi was impossible for me to do, and that I would never get it to harmonise with my body. But Mr. Yang was very good at karate, as I have said, and at Tai Chi as well. So I knew it could be done by others so therefore I could not stop. I would be in shame if I gave it up. This is why I kept at it; training, training and then more training. Still even after two years I was finding it hard. Then suddenly one day I was training, again, and I found some feeling. Ah, yes, this was it I thought to myself. It was only a small feeling in one part, but it was good, wonderful. After that I was able to concentrate much more on Tai Chi and began to like it very much."

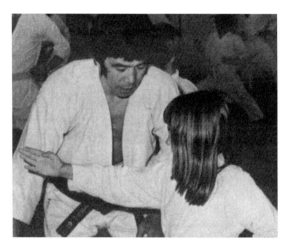

Kanazawa sensei helping a young student - from Karate & Oriental Arts magazine, January 1979.
Photograph:
John Van Weenen/Roger Carpenter

"But the Japanese mind some-times makes things difficult and this was such a situation. People would say to me, 'Why are you doing Tai Chi? You should concentrate on your karate. If you were doing this properly you would not have time to train in Tai Chi. If you have so much spare time, do more karate.' As a result of people saying things like this to me I did start training more in karate, but I also did my Tai Chi. I just never told people I was still doing it. It was my little secret with Mr. Yang."

Kanazawa sensei told me that he believes one should not try mixing the two arts together but they can be both studied with the idea of har-monising. Trying to mix the two arts will lead nowhere.

"You know I think that all karate-ka (karate students) would get some-thing from Tai Chi. Karate is all about getting stronger and stronger, but in time your body becomes weak as you grow old. This is the way of nature. There is nothing wrong with trying to be strong, but if you want to stay strong when you are old you must try to understand another way. Most people only come to understand the physical, external side of karate. They miss the internal side. Tai Chi is a very advanced internal technique, much more than karate I think."

"Even though the idea of ki or chi (internal energy) are the same, the two arts go about cultivating it in different ways. In Tai Chi you learn

about chi at the very beginning and you try to get the feeling, that is, the intention. But in karate it is not like that. You do not go into karate thinking about ki energy. I am speaking only personally here of course. Some teachers of karate may instruct their students about ki, from the start. But I don't know of any that do. In Tai Chi we try to harmonise our breathing with intention from inside our body in order to make chi. But it has to come naturally, not with forcing or making it happen."

"As you know, the old Okinawan masters learned their arts from China and so there are many links with Chinese martial arts philosophy and training methods. If you look, you can find these connections everywhere."

Before my interview came to an end, I wanted to return to the subject of Kanazawa sensei's feeling for karate, and in particular his teaching of kata from Goju-ryu. I had been wondering if it had anything to do with breathing methods, or if he saw Goju-ryu as some kind of bridge between the hardness of Shotokan and the softness of Tai Chi.

"Actually, in my opinion karate should not be thought of in terms of styles as such. You see, today a Shito-ryu teacher must teach only Shito-ryu techniques to his student, just as a Goju-ryu teacher must teach only the techniques of Goju-ryu. All the time, people are doing this so that they can pass on the techniques in the way they want them to be passed on. But I think, and I'm not sure what other teachers think, or if they would agree with me, that Shotokan for instance is very good for physical improvement of younger people. When you get a little older you need to pay attention to the 'tanden' (a point below the navel considered to be the centre of the body). This is more like Goju-ryu training. Older still, and Tai Chi is the best way to train. If you look at martial arts in this way you will see that training is not about which style you do. So I support the idea that when you are young you

Kanazawa sensei
with a hip powered
high punch - reach
and force!

Photograph; Karate
& Oriental Arts
magazine July 1981
- courtesy of
Shotokan Karate
International.

should train very hard. After about the age of thirty you should train more like the Goju-ryu way. I am talking only generally here because some people stay younger for longer. The main point is that you try to make you training match your age and ability."

I expect to train all my life. For me this is something I must do. My training has changed as I have grown older, in many ways. If this had not happened, when I hopefully reach seventy or eighty years old, many of the kata I did when I was young would be impossible. Even with kata from other karate traditions I am sure I would have trouble. But I know that I can do Tai Chi until I die, because it is more internal than external. Right now I am looking more inside for my training; less at the physical side of things. Internal training is good for my spirit; good also for my internal organs."

"To reiterate what I have said already, to emphasise it. The muscles predominate in importance when we want strength, and fast moving bodies. When the body muscles change with age, then you cannot rely on them in the same way and we need internal strength. Generally this happens in the thirties. After about fifty years old the internal organs begin to weaken, then you have to go to the power of your character, you have to go to spirit power. If your training has been correct up to that point, then your character and spirit will have grown stronger with the passing of the years."

"If you look at people you see how they can do things. You will see an example of what I mean. People who run short distances are best when they are younger, usually in their twenties. Middle distance runners are often better in their thirties. I think this is because when you run longer distances it is not just your body condition which does it but also there is something else; we can call it your mind if you like. Then if you look at the majority of people who do marathon runs, you will see that there are many older people who take part. It is a physical test of course, but I don't think they could do it if they were relying solely on muscle power and so forth."

As a final piece of advice from his vast experience, Kanazawa sensei told me that children should be taught how to breathe properly, and how to use their hips, and how to make correct stances. Later on they should be informed about the 'hara' (abdominal area) because a strong abdomen is needed to cultivate fighting spirit. He enlarged on this by saying that he was not just referring to fighting itself but to the efforts one must make to survive and endure in today' society.

"If you do not have this fighting spirit then you will not want to achieve anything in life. You will become lazy, and you will not want to study and work. You will not want to train yourself. Life is difficult so you must fight or struggle for what you want to achieve in it."

The last meeting with Kanazawa sensei took place at my home in October 1996. I had heard through the grapevine that he was coming to Perth and so I wasted no time in contacting his student there, Lex McKinly. Arrangements were made for him to bring Kanazawa sensei for lunch, after which I would once more interview him for magazines in Australia, England and the United States.

My wife and I had no idea when he would be arriving. That morning he had been conducting a national Dan grading for members of his Australian Shotokan Karate-do International Federation. Lex had promised to bring him at 'lunch time' but not knowing what this meant made it difficult to plan a hot meal. However within twenty minutes of their arrival we were sitting down to steaming hot food.

I had been looking forward to this visit from the first moment I had heard that Kanazawa sensei was coming. So when I heard the car pulling into the driveway I quickly slipped on my shoes and made my

way outside to greet them. Kanazawa sensei was already stepping out of the car when he first saw me, and at once smiled. he then bowed towards me and released a loud "Ouss". I returned his bow with an even deeper one. We shook hands warmly as we exchanged greetings and made polite enquiries about how each other had been in the years since we had last met.

"Is this the same house as before?" he asked while moving to the side of the driveway. Spotting my dojo standing in the back yard he answered his own question. "Ah, yes, so it is."

Over coffee we caught up on our respective lives and then Kanazawa sensei produced a silk neck tie that he had had made to commemorate the SKIF world championships in Japan. He presented it to me. I was humbled by the man's thoughtfulness and thanked him for his consideration towards me. I have to say that although this was not the first time a sensei of such standing has presented me with a gift, such events are sufficiently rare as to affect me deeply. Noticing my embarassment, Kanazawa sensei quickly moved the conversation on. When we sat down to lunch we continued to reminisce.

Lunch over, Kanazawa sensei, Lex and I retired to my study where the talk turned to some of the changes that sensei had introduced years ago when he was about to leave the J.K.A. (Japan Karate Association). It was about that time that Kanazawa sensei produced a book in which he talked about his approach to karate. It was an approach which he termed 'Shin' karate-do, or New karate-do. He said that he had been thinking about how and why we train the way we do. He explained.

"When you have a big association, it is very important to have a system of learning. Okay, I know this. But it seemed to me that the system taught students only to remember combinations. I wanted a sys-

tem which taught students to use their eyes and in fact their whole body, so they could respond to an attack from their own understanding."

I wondered if this had something to do for instance with his including mawashigeri (roundhouse kick) in the kata Empi. I asked him if he still trained in the kata this way. "Not any more," he said. "It was not the mawashigeri itself which mattered so much. I had simply noticed that we were using this kick a lot in jiyu-kumite (free style sparring). We also did it many times in kihon (basic technical training), so I wondered why it was not included in our kata. I wanted to have a kata where a student could use this kick. But it was more important that the student should realise that he could use this kick. There's a difference. I know that people were saying things about me; that I was changing the kata and that this was a bad thing. But you know, in the olden days this happened all the time. Kata must be of some help to a student and not just something separate from the rest of his training. Funakoshi sensei did the same thing when he changed mae-geri (front kick) to yoko-geri (side kick) in the Heian kata. Of course one should not change the kata just for the sake of changing it, but if the reason is good then in my opinion it is all right."

Listening to Kanazawa sensei speaking, it all made perfect sense, but at the same time I could not help but wonder about how many people would still miss the point of what he was saying, and how many would use his reasoning to explain away their own 'made up' kata. The conversation moved on to the subject of stances and why he was teaching his yudansha to use shiko-dachi as well as the usual kiba-dachi. This was to do with the same kind of thinking as bringing mawashigeri into a kata. As the Shotokan style did not use this stance as a rule, he said that he also had his senior students training in the Goju-ryu kata Seiyunchin and Sepai, because these are two kata which use this stance a lot.

Kanazawa sensei said that it was a question of balance. Kiba-dachi is very solid and strong, which is good for stability. However, Shiko-dachi allows for a little bit more flexibility for moving and also it is important to have both options open for the student. He added, "We need this flexibility, I think. We need it not just in the stance but in how our mind works."

He went on to explain that in nature, all things are an expression of Yin and Yang, and in his opinion it is important for a karate-ka to show this balance in his karate. Just being strong would solve only some problems, and being soft all the time would likewise provide answers to a limited range of circumstances. By bringing the two together in an attempt at harmony, it is possible to improve the situation. He went on.

"It is important to understand that even in strength there are many different types, and this is the same with being soft. Which is stronger, a rock or water? When I think of these stances I feel that the Shiko-dachi is more external, and pushing away, expanding myself. This is very hard for me to explain in English because my English is not so good. But I think that you can understand what I mean. So please explain to people what I am saying."

Although flattered that Kanazawa sensei had so much faith in me, I was not at all confident that I had the ability to translate his thoughts any better to the general public than his own statements had done, and this being the case I intend to leave it at that, and go on to some of the other points of interest that came up. I said that in my opinion, Shotokan was becoming a little softer in execution, and in many ways more subtle than it used to be. I added that I thought this has something to do with the age of the teachers who had first brought the style to the West. Kanazawa sensei said that in his view this was not the case. That Shotokan had always been a strong style, but that the way it looked depended entirely on the intentions of the person who was doing it. What age they were, and also their spirit and level of understanding (related to grade) were also relevant. Shotokan style has certain elements in it that cannot be left out. They have to be observed by everyone, and an example of this was the way to use the Tanden (lower abdominal region). He pointed out that without an understanding of such things one could not be said to be doing true Shotokan karate-do. Outwardly the style might look different, according to who was doing it, but inside there were a number of common things happening.

"Some people just want an easy life, and maybe this is why they do their kata slowly or too softly. If I see students doing this I say to them, 'No, no, go more quickly here, this must be stronger'. This is most important for kyu grade students to understand. Just do it. After Black Belt, okay, start thinking about why this is done this way, how can I make this work better for me, for my body. This way it is possible to develop a good 'feeling' about karate. At first if they work very hard they become tired, so okay, now they must think how can I stay strong without getting tired. If they continue to go slowly this is no good, this is not the answer. If they think about Shotokan they will understand how important the Tanden is, and it is here that they will find the answer."

The insight I was getting into the Shotokan style was a real education for me. I was beginning to see why some of the senior teachers of the style stand out from the main body of instructors. Like other human endeavours, karate was evolving. Thanks to Kanazawa sensei, I was having my eyes opened to that evolution. When I myself am teaching my students kumite, I stress the importance of making their Kamae part of their attack or defence. In other words they should set themselves up in such a way as to enhance their attacking moves, or likewise their defence and counter attack. How many

times have I seen someone standing in Kiba-dachi, completely sideways on to the opponent, and then spending his time lashing out with one leg? As a defence they seem only able to shift back, in crab fashion, out of range. The limitations of such a Kamae are obvious and to be wondered at, and I wondered what, if any, advice Kanazawa sensei might have to share on this point. He had!

"Yes, I agree with you," he replied. Kamae should be part of your technique. In the beginning, students should make a distinct Kamae. This is good as a basis for them to learn from. For higher grades, the best Kamae is no Kamae. For example if I make a Kamae like this (he shows one) you might be able to see a weakness, that is if you can attack. But then I might do the same thing on purpose, to invite you in, then 'bang' I hit you. You can also tell if someone is frightened, by the Kamae he or she makes. You can see confidence too. For competition it is better to find a Kamae which will give you a good possibility of winning, whether you are attacking or defending."

The conversation flowed on to the subject of a person's weaknesses, and how in Japanese karate this is known as "suki", which means 'opening'. Three 'suki' are recognised. These are 'Kokoro no 'suki'', 'Kamae no 'suki'' and 'Waza no 'suki''. The first has to do with one's mind or one's concentration. Kanazawa sensei explained that if you mind is not on your opponent, but wanders on to something else, you are bound to lose. If your mind is full of thoughts, or you are worried, this is also 'suki'. So we can say that one form of 'suki' is distraction. He emphasised that a clear head is most important. Kamae no 'suki' refers to an opening in one's guard or Kamae. Such a 'suki' leaves one open to an attack. So since this too is connected with one's state of concentration it is linked to Kokoro no 'suki'. The third example, Waza no 'suki', is when a technique is not performed correctly, or performed weakly. For instance a lack of "hikite", bad balance, poor breathing and no kime all are instances of Waza no 'suki'. Kanazawa sensei said that senior students should be looking at all these things when they are training.

As a western student of karate, the words I heard more and more from my Japanese teachers were, "Use your hips". In fact these words I heard more than any others. Often I went home after training with these words ringing in my ears. This prompted me to want to speak about them, and in particular the notion of "koshi". As I understood it, 'koshi' had to do less with twisting the hips and more to do with pushing them. It also suggested the idea of using all of your body to kick. So I asked Kanazawa sensei about this term 'koshi' and he replied as follows.

"'Koshi' means that you must use your Hara. Sometimes some people use the word and they are talking about twisting your hips. But I think 'koshi' is a little different from this. The feeling you have with 'koshi' is to bring your Hara and your kick together at the same time. This will give more power to your kick. It is not just a technique but a feeling too." When I heard this I saw that it would lead to the next topic I wanted to bring up, which was the difference between 'Bunkai' and 'oyo'. As I believe that Bunkai is an explanation of the move found in kata, and 'oyo' to be an expression of a person's understanding of the principles found in a kata, I wondered how Kanazawa sensei saw it. He said.

"Bunkai is a way of explaining what the meaning is behind the kata techniques; what does each move mean? And so when you train in Bunkai you stay close to the movement found in the kata. But with 'oyo' the movement from the kata is used to show the idea. Therefore when you are training in 'oyo' your movement carries on from the idea in the kata. Often the kata might stop at some point and move from the present attacker to another attacker. But when doing 'oyo' you would continue until you brought the opponent under control.

'oyo' comes more from your feelings and how well you understand the lesson the kata was teaching. Bunkai is just an explanation to help give a clearer picture of the kata."

As the afternoon wore on, we touched upon other subjects such as the need from time to time for a student to 'Plough his Spirit', and how it is necessary to develop the mind as well as the body. How developing one's own fate was as important as the realisation that studying the martial arts is a never ending process. From such a man as Kanazawa sensei it is possible to learn many things.

Before we went across to my dojo, I asked him how his own hombu was faring, now that it had been open for some time. "Well, you know, it is going very well. It is close to the railway station so it is convenient for people. It is open every day and we have a number of different instructors there. We also rent it out to a number of different groups who do not have premises of their own and need such a building. When they are using it we have training at our Tokyo hombu in the Yoyogi district. So now if a student comes from overseas, he or she can train every day at either the Tokyo or International hombu. I have been able to cut down on the amount of travelling I am doing, and so now I am in Japan for more than half the year."

I wanted to ask Kanazawa sensei what training he did for himself these days. It was important for me to ask this before our conversation came to an end. Being so far from my own sensei, and having a dojo in my home where I could train every day, I hoped to get some pointers from him. This may sound an attractive situation to be in, but sometimes it takes a good chunk of imagination to get myself motivated. Kanazawa sensei's answer was not what I was expecting. He began.

"First of all when I wake up, I train for one hour in my bed. I do many

movements with different muscle groups, and roll my eyes in different ways. If anyone were to see me doing all this, they could be excused for thinking that I was mad. Then I meditate to settle my mind, ready for the day. Then I concentrate on different parts of my body, like the heart, or lungs, and do breathing training. Every day I also do "komon" training. ('komon' is the Japanese word for anus.) This is very important as you get older. Many people have trouble with this part of the body. If you do karate you must always be thinking about how to look after yourself, and if you don't, then one day you will have to stop. I am trying to be ready for training when I'm ninety years old, or maybe even older."

"Not long ago I was teaching in the Caribbean, when the area was hit by a very large hurricane. It was really powerful and there was a lot of damage, and people died. Then about two weeks later, after I had returned to Japan, I found myself in the middle of another big storm. This brought about massive flooding, and again some people were killed. A few times I wondered if I myself could have died in either of these storms. Although I had been excited and even a little nervous, I was never frightened. A karate person must be ready for anything, even death. I'm not saying you should look for such things, but you should be ready for whatever life might send your way."

Who could argue with that, I thought, and then wondered immediately if I myself was ready for anything. The honest answer was that I was probably not ready. I saw it as an indicator that I needed more training. Our far ranging interview moved for a while to Kanazawa sensei's earlier years of training, and in particular to the time he spent on Okinawa, home of karate-do. He spoke of this period with obvious affection. It brought back happy memories for him. Especially strong were his feelings for the time when he stood in the back yard dojo of the late Master Yuchoku Higa sensei of the Shorin-ryu. As he watched the master hitting the makiwara, he could not help but notice

how the master's fist seemed to land on a different part of the straw target with each punch. This, he remembers thinking, was shockingly bad for a karate-ka, in terms of a demonstration of skill or focus. After all, having good focus and being able to hit the same spot on the makiwara over and over again was something all good Dan grades could do, let alone a person who is considered a master.

It was only after some twenty minutes of watching, that it dawned on the young Japanese just what was really going on. Instead of being sloppy, as Kanazawa sensei had mistakenly believed, Higa sensei was in fact aiming for each corner in turn and then placing his fifth punch exactly in the centre. He was doing this at high speed and with great power.

"It was me," he explained. "I could not understand at first what I was seeing. When I did realise what he was doing I was of course impressed by his ability. I felt somewhat ashamed by my own initial failure to see it. That was a big lesson for me. Later Higa sensei gave a big smile. He knew that I had understood his lesson. He said that not all students learn such lessons, which require observation and appreciation; however, by learning as I had, I had shown that I could go far into karate-do. This expression of my potential by such a veteran of our art made me feel very happy."

As he finished speaking, I wondered if it was this kind of capacity which had permitted Kanazawa sensei to embrace not only karate-do but also Tai Chi and Ko-Budo (weapons arts). Although Shotokan is not my style, I can honestly say that he has been a teacher for me. In the many years of our relationship, he has always been generous with his time and knowledge, and shown me the kind of consideration which always leaves me feeling humbled.

Now, at sixty-nine years of age, Kanazawa sensei is a fine example

to all Budo-ka. This is true not only in the way he approaches his martial arts but more importantly in the way he approaches life. If ever you have the chance to train with him I advise you to take it. One of the other things we spoke about that afternoon was the concept of "kaiun", developing your own fate. Kanazawa sensei is a great believer in making the things you want happen. As he had said to me once before:

"Life is difficult, so you must fight for what you want to achieve in it."

Controlling Others by Controlling Yourself
The jujutsu of Jan De Jong

By anyone's standards, Jan De Jong sensei is an impressive man. (pronounced: Yan De Yong). This is not because of any physical attributes nor because of an overly forceful character. Rather it is due to his 'presence'. When I met him he was in his seventies. He was a very easy person to relax with and went out of his way to encourage this in me.

As a master of jujutsu, De Jong sensei has been around long enough to see most things come and go. For the first time in a long time I had the feeling that here was a man who was really at peace with himself. Indeed he told me, "I make a point of not worrying about anything". In the summer of 1994 I spent a very pleasant afternoon as a guest in his home in the western suburbs of Perth, Western Australia. As always on such occasions as this, the time passed far too quickly and in the few hours I was there I was able to grasp only a little, of course, of what this man had to offer in the way of knowledge. With over sixty years of martial arts training behind him, that knowledge is extensive, as is his personal library of books and video tapes. I noticed also, for it was hard not to do so, that he still retains his enthusiasm; not only for jujutsu, but also for silat, and other martial arts.

Here then was a man who is the living embodiment of the adage, 'Walk quietly, but carry a big stick'. His gentle character does ensure that he walks quietly through life, but one only has to see him executing the techniques of jujutsu to realise that he carries within him far more striking power than that of merely a big stick. As he said to me several times in the course of our conversation, "First you must learn to control yourself, and then you can learn to control others". This is his basic philosophy and he is at pains to teach it to his many students.

The De Jong family (l. to r.):
son Hans, wife Margaret, De Jong sensei, daughter Maggie
Photograph - author.

As his name suggests, De Jong sensei is Dutch. When I first met him I expected our conversation to be about his time training in the art of jujutsu. But events proved otherwise. He was born in Holland and as a small boy moved to Sumarang in Java, where his father was taking up a post on a plantation. At that time, the area now known as Indonesia, was under the rule of the Netherlands, or Holland, and known as the Dutch East Indies. De Jong sensei grew up there, did all his schooling there, and regarded the place as his home.

His first introduction to martial arts was through his father, who trained in jujutsu under two Japanese who were living in Sumarang. "I was very lucky," he told me. "It was only a small dojo, and apart

from my father and a few of his friends, the rest of the students were Japanese. Both sensei were called Saito; they were brothers. One worked as a florist and the other as a photographer. I trained with them for fourteen years and learned a lot from them. The style of jujutsu was Tsutsumi-ryu."

"It was founded my master Tsutsumi who had studied the style of Takenouchi jujutsu. The elder Saito sensei had been a student of master Tsutsumi and was graded to 7th Dan by him. By the time I left the dojo I myself was 3rd Dan."

"The style of Tsutsumi-ryu is a very well balanced one, making it good for self defence. There are five types of body movements: sweeping, gliding and flowing used mainly for escaping, and then the entering and entering rotation movements. All these ways of moving have many variations, and you would use them depending on what is happening to you at the time. There is also a lot of work done unbalancing the attacker. Once again this depends on how you are being attacked as to which techniques you would use, for instance the same side or the reverse. The block you might use would come from one of six groups of blocks. These are: stopping, sweeping, pushing, grabbing, pulling and empty blocking."

"Once you have an attacker under control you can move to 'finish him off' in a number of ways. These would include taking him to the floor and controlling there, choking him, striking him or throwing him. As always though, the response you use should be in accordance with how you are attacked. Just from this basic outline you can see that there is a lot to learn. Of course once you have learned these techniques you have to train hard to keep them polished and in working order."

Being in the right place at the right time through 'tai sabaki' (body shifting) is one sure way of allowing you to deal with an attacker, however De Jong sensei was not always able to judge things as finely as he does today. He left home as a young man and went back to Holland to finish his education. Once this was over he planned to study to become a pilot. No sooner had he arrived in Europe than the tide of the German army washed over the continent and occupied the Netherlands. Survival became the name of the game.

He was no longer able to receive financial help from his father, and was forced to borrow money from family and friends. He realised that this could not continue indefinitely, and no one had the remotest idea how long the war would last. Then one day he met a man called Rienier Hulsk who was running a sports club. By all accounts he was a very good businessman and saw in De Jong sensei the opportunity to feed a growing need in the population. Hulsk spoke encouragingly to the young De Jong. "Look, now that the Germans are here we have the black-out, the black market and the underground (Dutch resistance fighters). Everyone lives in fear. You have a black belt in jujutsu so how about teaching self defence at my school?"

What the man was saying was the truth. The civilian population lived in fear of their lives, and even a trip to buy food could end in disaster. With no other obvious way open to him to make money, De Jong sensei started teaching jujutsu. After the first year he decided to open his own school and within a few months he had over three hundred students enrolled. He never asked the Germans what they thought about this. Nor were the students, I suppose, in a mad rush to tell them about it either. Of note is the fact that much later De Jong sensei noticed how strong the populations of all the occupied countries were in judo or jujutsu. Denmark, Norway, Belgium, France and of course Holland were all very strong in this respect, and realistic too. After the war things began to change and this he believes was due to the introduction of a strong competitive element, where the sport of judo was emphasised. Now he considers that these coun-

De Jong sensei applying neck and shoulder lock.

Photograph - author.

tries are no longer the home of realistic fighting methods. When I asked him if he could go into details about what life was like in Holland during the occupation he replied,

"Well you know it's not a time I really like to dwell on. War is such madness, not to mention stupidity, and it turns people into creatures that do such horrible things to others. But I can tell you a story from that period, when I actually used my jujutsu, then we'll leave it at that."

"One day the Germans decided to round up all the local able bodied young men and ship them off to Germany for slave labour. As you can imagine I did not want to got but under the circumstances I had no choice! So there I was with hundreds of others standing on a train in the middle of the night. It was pitch black. The windows of the train had been painted over so there wasn't even any moonlight by which to see. We were packed into the train like sardines in a can as we

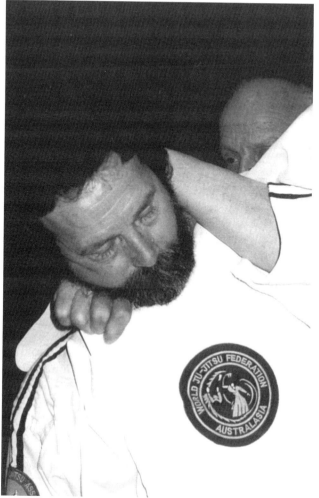

Close-up of necklock

Photograph - author.

waited to move off. There was a German soldier on guard at every door. After a time I felt I had to go to the toilet. My discomfort grew and grew until I couldn't hold it in any more. There was no way the guard was going to let me off the train or anything as considerate as that, so I worked my way towards the door. All the time I was stumbling, really just hoping I was moving in the right direction."

"My situation was desperate, so I gave up the notion of reaching the door and turned simply to the wall. I was going to urinate down the inside of my long overcoat. This way I thought I would cause the least inconvenience to everyone else packed into the carriage. What I didn't know was that I was unwittingly relieving myself over a German guard who was sitting at the door. I had in fact blindly navigated successfully. The first thing I knew about this was a yell from the guard, then shouting and cursing at me in German. His flashlight came on and in a panic I headed for the door itself to

escape. As I reached it I felt his hand grab me on the shoulder. Without thinking I turned, seized his hand and threw him to the floor as hard as I could. He didn't move. I quickly left the train. My heart was pounding so hard it seemed that it would leap out of my chest. I hid until the train left a short time later. As the guard didn't raise the alarm I assumed that I must have knocked him out."

As this tale came to an end I realised that De Jong sensei did not want to speak any more about life under the Germans, so I moved the conversation forward to the years after the war.

"When the war was over I didn't want to stay in Europe. For one thing it was too cold compared with Java, there was rationing, things were disrupted and in short everything was in a mess. Anyway I decided to return to Java. A friend of my father's was an officer in the Dutch army and he found me a job as a physiotherapist in the Dutch Indonesian Army. Unfortunately for my plans, by the time I returned to Java there was another war going on. This time it was between the Dutch and the Indonesians who were fighting for their independence. I did not welcome this, as you can imagine. War is a terrible thing. In the end of course, independence came."
I wondered how this period in his life had affected or contributed to his study of martial arts.

"In my school days growing up in Java, I had seen little bits of the native fighting arts, notably and mostly silat. I played around with the local boys, but this was not serious training. Now I became interested in it again and so I thought about going into it properly."

"I had this chap who used to come to our house to cut my hair. One day we got to talking about silat. I asked him if he knew of a good teacher, a 'guru' who might teach me. He replied that he did know someone who was well informed about silat and that he would bring him to see me. So my barber brought his friend a couple of times and on each visit he would talk about the art, but there was never any suggestion of my training with him or even visiting his school. On one of these occasions he brought with him a second man called Suhadi. Over the next months, Suhadi would drop in and talk to me about this and that. One day he asked me, 'Why do you want to do silat? You're white, you should be doing tennis or something like that.' I told him that it was my heart that wanted to do silat, and that I had always been interested in Indonesian art and culture. This was how I saw silat too, and this was why I wanted to train in it."

"Suhadi's visits continued and then again some months later he asked me if I was still interested. Of course replied that I was. He then said, 'Okay, from now on I am your guru.' At first I was not sure what he was talking about, but as it turned out he was not only a teacher of silat, but the chief guru for the whole of middle Java. In all the previous months he had never mentioned that he was a guru, or even knew silat. He had spent the time testing me and testing my sincerity. I should mention that he had sometimes brought along with him other men to see me, and these were in fact other gurus from the district. I realised that I had so to speak been on display, been subjected without my knowledge to a type of guru court, judging my suitability."

"This may now seem like a long drawn out process. But even the local people who wanted to train in silat had to go through a similar procedure. A candidate would be asked to go and visit a certain person in some village. Then he would be asked by that person to go and see yet another person in another village. This type of thing would go on until the teachers were happy that the prospective student was sincere, earnest. Because I was Dutch, and white, Suhadi was not happy about me going to certain villages; he did not think it was safe. So he brought gurus to see me instead."

"After I had been training for about a month, I handed my guru an envelope with some money in it. This was a token of my appreciation for his instruction. Then one month later I did the same thing. This time he looked at me and asked what was in the envelope. He said, 'Is this the same as last time?' I told him it was. He then gave me back the envelope and told me never to do such a thing again. 'We do not teach for money,' he said. 'However, should one of your brothers (in silat) need help, we will expect you to assist him if you can.' This is the way payment was made for your training. Every now and then I was asked to help out with some things for one or two people, and I was happy to do so."

In 1952 De Jong sensei moved to Australia. His memories of those early days in Perth, the most isolated English speaking city in the world, are not fond ones.

"Perth was not the big, modern city it is today. In fact back in the early fifties it was a backward place. Do you know I couldn't even get a Chinese meal here. There were about three Italian restaurants and that was it. I started to teach jujutsu on the hill, in front of the Western Australia parliament building. After a year or two, some of the students got together and found a place to train. It was the Swan river rowing club's clubhouse. So from 1955 onwards I was teaching classes there. We moved again, but after that second move I found the building where my dojo is now. We have been there for nearly thirty years.

"Back in 1955 I had ten students, but no mats to train on. One day I was demonstrating what we call a 'bridge fall' when both my legs crashed through the floor boards. That's when I definitely decided to get mats! For a long time I taught only jujutsu. I did have a small number of students to whom I taught silat, but I did this only to maintain my own level of training. Nevertheless I wasn't too keen to teach silat to westerners at that time. What I did was to wait and see if someone could apply himself really well to jujutsu. I looked to see if I could find people with really good character and attitude. If I found one I would ask him if he would like to study silat. So in this way I got only a few students at a time."

By the mid-sixties I was being asked all the time to teach silat. At first I told people they had to train in jujutsu first. But in the end I decided to teach silat to the general public. I placed an advertisement in the newspaper and to my great surprise on the day of the classes there were queues of people all the way down the street. Many of the people who are top karate practitioners in Perth today started with me back then. These classes really took off, but I found that I had to modify things a little for the Australian students. You see in Indonesia you have to have a lot of patience. They have a different set of values from the Australians, so I changed the way I

De Jong sensei demonstrating a wrist and armlock.

Photograph - author.

taught to suit them, and by doing so I got them to understand what I was trying to teach."

This seemed something of a questionable thing to do, changing things to suit the students, so I asked De Jong sensei to explain what he meant by this. He replied.

"Yes, I know what you're saying, but you can learn in many different ways, and if one way gives better results than another, why carry on in a way that gives poorer results? Let me give you an example of what I mean. Back in 1978 Major Greg Mawkes, M.B.E., of the Australian army, asked me if I would teach self defence techniques to the Commandoes and the Australian Special Air Service. Shortly after I started teaching, the Major and I had a progress meeting. He said that he was very pleased with the fighting method, but told me that his troops were having difficulty understanding it all.

I reassured him that this was the usual way of things, and explained that my own students were the same. He got the point but said to me that the army did not have unlimited time to spend on this, and that they needed quick results."

"So it was after that meeting that I had to think things through and see how I could impart the same amount of understanding by other than traditional ways. The first thing I did was to have a look at how the army go about teaching other subjects. From what I gleaned from this I brought my own methods more into line with theirs. Well it wasn't long before people began to understand things better and therefore do the techniques better than before. After that I held a meeting with my instructors and suggested that we teach all of the students in the same way. The techniques remained the same of course, and it was only the method that was different. Since then things have been much better."

Today in his mid-seventies, De Jong sensei retains a personal schedule which would leave behind many half his age. Mondays, Wednesdays and Fridays he teaches privately in a dojo he built in the garden of his home. Here also his instructors gather twice a week at six in the morning for a training session before heading off to work. In addition he teaches twice a week at his main dojo in Perth's city centre.

Each year he receives many requests from jujutsu-ka around the world by letter, fax and email. The demand is so high that De Jong sensei annually leaves Perth and embarks on a teaching tour around the world. Then he also teaches in other places in Australia, and given the size of the country this involves as much travelling as would a tour of Europe.

As a final question I asked him what he thought was the value of training in the martial arts these days. He replied that proper training would bring self control. He reminded me that in order to control others we first have to learn control of ourselves. This is important, he emphasised, and applies to people of all ages.

Obeying the Way of Spiritual Law
Eiichi Miyazato's Jundokan

There are those who think of karate as nothing more than a sport. Such people, however long they train, never come to understand the true depth and value of the tradition they 'dabble' in. This way of thinking could not have been further from the way Miyazato sensei saw things. Born in July in 1922 in Naha, Okinawa's capital, Miyazato sensei began training in karate fourteen years later under master Chojun Miyagi, the founder of Goju-ryu karate-do.

At that time, and in common with other teachers of karate-do in Okinawa, Master Miyagi taught his students in his back yard. Miyazato sensei remembered that it was a well equipped dojo, with makiwara (punching boards), chi-ishi (strength building stones - weights) and all the other tools used in the practice of Hojo-Undo (supplementary training). Students numbers were never high, usually around ten, and this Miyazato sensei said was because the training regime was so hard. Miyagi sensei was known as a real task master. He did not like his students to ask questions. He preferred that they simply worked hard and discovered things for themselves. Above all, Master Miyagi stressed that humility should be the aim of all of his deshi (karate students).

In those early days when personal transport usually meant walking or catching a ride on a horse and cart if you were lucky, attendance at the dojo was limited for some students to only a few days each month. The fortunate few who lived close by had the luxury of practising every day. The dojo was open each day from six in the morning until ten at night. Although there were no set classes, the work rate of each student was kept high by the ever present figure of Master Miyagi. Neither the students nor their teacher wore the traditional karate-gi

A youthful Miyazato sensei being blocked by his teacher Master Miyagi.

Photograph - E. Miyazato

(uniform) universally worn today. Students used to arrive, remove their shirts, roll up their trousers and simply start training. It was only later, shortly before Master Miyagi died that he took to wearing a gi. Miyazato sensei believed that this was done more to fall in line with karate's acceptance into the Japanese martial arts world than for any practical reason.

Often the sessions would begin with a run around the Tsuboya district. On their return, students would engage in stretching and strengthening exercises, before moving on to conditioning with the hojo-undo tools. I was told that this was done in order to make the students strong and their techniques real. Miyazato sensei said that Master Miyagi would make them repeat Sanchin kata over and over, many times. By today's standards, I guess that one might say that this method of training could prove a little boring for those other than the most dedicated. However, such was the strength of feeling that Miyazato sensei had for his teacher, that any thoughts of giving up his

Master Chojun Miyagi escapes from the grip of his student Miyazato sensei.

Photograph - E. Miyazato

training were never seriously countenanced. In one breath Miyazato sensei told me that his teacher was a hard task master and also how kind he was to his students. The love which Miyazato sensei had for his teacher was evident, even though he had died over forty years earlier.

He remembered Ji'nan Shinzato sensei, also with great fondness. This man would have succeeded Master Miyagi, had he not been killed in the battle for Okinawa towards the end of the war against Japan. "Shinzato sensei," Miyazato sensei recalled, "was Master Miyagi's favourite student, and he would have taken over from him, had not the war taken him from us."

As the years passed, the bond between student and teacher grew, and only when Miyazato sensei was called to military duty in the

Japanese army did he leave the dojo. He was absent for three years and when he returned it was to a scene of devastation. In 1945 Okinawa was considered by the Allied Command to be the gateway to Japan. Just three hundred and fifty miles from the mainland, it was crucial to American strategy, a vital position from which they could launch air attacks and gather forces for the final invasion. The battle for Okinawa took three months and in the end was one of the bloodiest conflicts of the whole Pacific campaign. It was here that the kamikaze suicide pilots made their first appearance, attacking the United States naval forces over one thousand nine hundred times. When the troops finally made it on to the island it was found that the loss of life had been much greater than anyone anticipated, with American personnel suffering some fifty thousand casualties. Okinawan civilian casualties were estimated to be over one hundred and sixty thousand during the period it took to secure Okinawa. Little wonder then that training in karate was very low on the list of priorities for those who had survived the warfare. Koshin Iha sensei, another of

Eichi Miyazato sensei.

Photograph - E. Miyazato

Master Miyagi's students from that period, said that Okinawa looked like the face of the moon when the fighting was over. People were living from hand to mouth, with little shelter or clothing. Food shops were empty, money was in short supply.

Gradually, life began to return to some kind of normality and people moved slowly back to living in ways which they had followed for centuries. Part of this return was the emergence of some karate teachers who had survived. They began to impart their knowledge again to the small band of students who gathered around them. When Miyazato sensei returned to Okinawa, Master Miyagi advised him on what to do.

"He brought me to police headquarters, where he was teaching karate. He found me a position as a judo teacher. (Miyazato sensei was also a highly ranked judo-ka.) Then I began to receive extra instruction in Goju-ryu. When Master Miyagi was away I taught the karate classes too. The training methods there were different in small ways from those of Master Miyagi's home dojo, but the techniques were the same."

I asked what, if anything, Master Miyagi emphasised when he taught. Miyazato sensei replied. "As I recall we first concentrated on becoming fit and strong , but the main point in Master Miyagi's teaching was in the kata. We would spend many hours training in kata, over and over. Of course this was not just in the forms but also in the bunkai (applications, meanings, interpretations). When we were strong and well conditioned, then the bunkai entered our training. The longer we trained the more complex and subtle the bunkai became. I want to warn people not to get the two things mixed up; kata is one thing and bunkai another. We used the kata to hide the bunkai. There are many confusing things done in the kata to hide the bunkai. For instance in the kata Saifa, when you block the arm and catch the leg,

Commemorative bust of Goju-ryu Founder, Master Chojun Miyagi with
(l. to r.) Seikichi Toguchi sensei, Eiichi Miyazato sensei, Meitoku Yagi sensei
and the sculptor of the bust.

in the kata you look left and then right but in the bunkai you do not
do this. You face your attacker. This type of thing is found in kata, all
kata. So many people practise kata but do not understand it. If you
don't understand the bunkai you will never learn the real meaning of
kata."

"We are all different in shape and size. Therefore, it is important that
each person understands the kata so that he or she can adjust it to
the particular body. This is part of the way we make the techniques
practical. So if follows from this that it is okay to change the moves
a little to suit your body. But when we teach the kata to students, we

must pass it on in the correct, original form, to the best of our ability. We must not pass on our own modified form if we can help it. If we don't pass on the correct form to the next generation, the kata will soon change beyond recognition from the one handed down to us. Teach the kata the correct way and adjust it only for oneself. Also as you get older it is natural to adjust the kata and practise it your own way. When you reach fifty, sixty or seventy years, you find you have to make changes. That's okay."

Miyazato sensei observes a student's kata performance.

Photograph - author.

"I am talking here about people who have been training for many years. That is, people who have made changes in their kata from their understanding of Goju-ryu. Some people do in fact try to change things too soon, before they know what they are doing. In the kata Sanchin for instance, many people do it far too quickly. This kata should, on the contrary, be performed slowly and with concentration. So what sometimes happens, and very frequently, is that people focus on the upper half of their bodies and forget almost completely about their legs and feet. In Sanchin kata the whole body has to be made strong, not just the top half. The feet should grip the floor. When pulling the arms back, care should be taken not to lift the shoulders or allow the elbows to stick out at the sides."

Miyazato sensei readily admitted that the Okinawans changed the fighting techniques which were brought in from China, to suit their own physiques and mentalities. But as far as he is able to ascertain, the techniques and method which were handed down to master Miyagi from his teacher, master Kanryo Higaonna, have changed very little. "All of Master Higaonna's Naha-te method can be found in today's Goju-ryu. Because of his personal feelings for certain things, master Higaonna's karate may have looked a bit different, but the feelings for what you are doing are still the same."

I asked about other styles of karate who use Goju-ryu kata in their practise. "They use the kata but it is not Goju-ryu karate-do. You see if you use the movements differently from how they were intended, then you are doing something else, not Goju-ryu. Only those people who are making a study of Goju-ryu kata and karate are training in the tradition of my teacher Master Miyagi. For an example take Shito-ryu karate where they use some Goju-ryu kata. The founder of that style, Mabuni sensei, trained alongside my teacher under Master Kanryo Higaonna, but he trained for a short period only; just a few years, and that's all. He studied also with Master Itosu who taught a different

type of karate. When Mabuni sensei left for Japan he started to teach a karate style that was a mixture of both Naha-te and Shuri-te. he put his own feelings and meanings into his karate. That's okay to do, but it meant that the feelings for the kata had been changed from the ones handed down to him. So the situation is that Shito-ryu people do our kata, but it cannot be said to be Goju-ryu."

Miyazato sensei continued to teach in the same way he was taught by master Miyagi. Each student was given the type of information which he needed at the time, according to his level of understanding. Even a lesson on the same point would differ from student to student. This way, everyone worked to his limit.

This approach comes from the old days when there were few students, and the sensei's aim was to bring out the very best in each of them. I remember thinking at the time he told me this, that such an approach has no place in today's world of commercial dojos with their professional instructors. Personally I feel that we are the poorer today because of the approach that most schools have adopted. Be that as it may, this is the world as it is now, and if the martial arts have any value they will survive.

When master Chojun Miyagi died in October 1953, the fate of Goju-ryu lay in the balance. Although many had tasted the style he had created, few students knew it well enough to really continue the tradition. The senior student at the Miyagi dojo was Miyazato sensei, and at the request of both the Miyagi family and the other students he took on the responsibility of teaching. He felt the pressure of his responsibility very keenly, and for a while there was some concern that the legacy left by his teacher might fade and die.

"When sensei died I was given all the training equipment and asked to continue teaching at the dojo in his backyard. This was a very difficult time for all of us. After a while some students began to come. I continued with my training there for the next three years, then I opened my own dojo, the Jundokan. On one level this means that my dojo is the next dojo to come after Master Miyagi's, but on a deeper level it means that I am complying with the way of spiritual law. We need this spiritual law, this morality. If we have this we will never be defeated, even if we lose a fight."

The Jundokan dojo has been open for over forty years and over these years many people have been trained by Miyazato sensei in the tradition of Goju-ryu. He always tried to get students to find the meanings within kata for themselves, and that through this, kata and bunkai, they would come to understand the Goju-ryu style. He encouraged students to look at other martial arts and to learn from them. When teaching, he took into account not only their karate ability but also their occupation and marital status, believing that karate should come third in a student's life, after family and work. Furthermore, he felt that students should enjoy karate, and that serious training and hard training should not stifle this enjoyment.

"You must train you body and mind together, not just your body. Strive to make your karate practical, simple, not complicated. Keep your mind on the dojo-kun (a set of precepts found in all traditional dojo). If you do this, you will not stray far from the right pursuit of understanding karate-do."

The dojo-kun hanging on the wall in the Jundokan reads as follows:

(Although exact translation is perhaps not possible the message that the dojo-kun delivers is clear. Throughout it we can see that the students are required to be honest with both themselves and others. Miyazato sensei said that this particular set of kun have come from the way Master Miyagi taught his students.)

First - be humble and polite

First - train considering your physical strength

First - practice earnestly with creativity

First - be calm and swift

First - take care of your health

First - live a plain life

First - do not be too proud or too modest

First - continue training with patience

In 1955, less than two years after the death of Master Miyagi, a general meeting of the students of Goju-ryu was held at a restaurant in Matsuo in Naha. Chairman for the meeting was Genkai Nakaima, a long time student of the late master. Once the meeting had been brought to order, the chairman explained the current status of the Miyagi dojo and that of the small association that existed at the time. He also wanted the assembly to publicly recognise the successor to Master Miyagi and to this end he moved a motion to recommend Miyazato sensei, as it had been he who had carried on the teaching at the Miyagi dojo. There was only one objection from the floor, and this was on the basis that Miyazato sensei had spent a lot of time studying judo. The chairman then asked if there was anyone who would like to recommend someone else. The assembled meeting remained silent. Keiyo Madanbashi sensei then moved the motion that since no one had an opinion on who else should be proposed to succeed Miyagi sensei, maybe they could try to find out from the Miyagi family if Master Miyagi himself had ever expressed a preference. At that point, Mr. Kin Miyagi, the late Master's second son, was consulted about this. He told the assembled people that his father had been saying for some time that Eiichi, that is Miyazato sensei, was the only one upon whom he could rely after his death. When this information had been absorbed, the chairman repeated his question if anyone objected to his proclaiming Miyazato sensei as the successor to Master Miyagi. There were no takers. Miyazato sensei was then recognised as the head of Goju-ryu and successor to their late teacher. Everyone applauded and the meeting came to an end.

Since that time Miyazato sensei has carried on in the same tradition as the one set by his teacher. When I last saw him at a small restaurant not far from the Jundokan, he spoke to me of training with an honest heart. He took some paper and a pen, and wrote two kanji - Chinese characters - which, when read together, said, 'Follow your heart'.

When he left a little later, he turned just before walking through the door. "Don't forget," he said.

I had no idea that this would be my final meeting with my sensei. In the summer of 1999 he was admitted to hospital but recovered well enough to continue his daily training. So it came as a great shock when I received a phone call from Okinawa on the night of December 11th that year, informing me of Miyazato sensei's death. Of all the

teachers I have had, he was the most traditional. His warm heart, hidden by a somewhat gruff exterior, is sadly missed by those of us who called him sensei.

CONCLUSION

It is possible for everyone who embarks upon the 'Way', the middle path through life, to reach the top of his or her own mountain. But the road is hard and the journey long. Only a few will succeed. It is the journey itself which brings rewards to those of us who are willing to try.

Over the time in which I have been trying to progress, I have met not only those masters who appear in the book, but others who have helped me to find the way towards the top of my personal mountain. One day I hope to be able to help others who have made less progress than I. In this way the spirit of Budo will pass from one generation to another.

If the day ever dawns which finds me standing at the summit of my own mountain, I pray that I will have the presence of mind to remember all those who gave so much of themselves to bring me to that spot. The generosity of spirit I have already received from them has lifted me higher than I could have managed had I been relying solely on my own ability. Should you find yourself the recipient of similar generosity, do not forget to offer your thanks before passing on your way.